That Patchwork Place®

AROUND THE BLOCK Again

More Rotary-Cut Blocks

from Judy Hopkins

Contents

CREDITS

President . . . . Nancy J. Martin
CEO . . . . Daniel J. Martin
Publisher . . . . Jane Hamada
Editorial Director . . . . Mary V. Green
Editorial Project Manager . . . . Tina Cook
Design and Production Manager . . . . Stan Green
Cover Designer . . . . Trina Stahl
Text Designer . . . . Kay Green
Technical Editor . . . . Ursula Reikes
Copy Editor . . . . Leslie Phillips
Illustrator . . . . Laurel Strand

Around the Block Again: More Rotary-Cut Blocks from
Judy Hopkins
© 2000 by Judy Hopkins

That Patchwork Place is an imprint of Martingale & Company.

Martingale & Company
PO Box 118
Bothell, WA 98041-0118
www.patchwork.com

MISSION STATEMENT

We are dedicated to providing quality products and service by working together to inspire creativity and to enrich the lives we touch.

Printed in China
05 04 03 02 01 00   8 7 6 5 4 3 2 1

Library of Congress Cataloging-in-Publication Data
Hopkins, Judy.
   Around the block again / by Judy Hopkins.
     p. cm.
   ISBN 1-56477-265-9
     1. Quilting—Patterns. I. Title.
   TT835.H5573 2000
   746.46'041—dc21
                                         00-063797

Introduction

Like many quiltmakers, I work primarily with the pieced block, drawing inspiration from our rich heritage of traditional design. My fondness for traditional patterns goes hand in hand with an unwavering commitment to quick, contemporary cutting techniques. I am a busy woman, and there are lots of quilts I want to make!

The storehouse of traditional designs is vast, but in many ways it is not accessible to today's mainstream quilter. While there are numerous block books on the market, many of them are reference books, geared toward pattern identification. They are tantalizing collections of possibilities that are out of reach of the quilter who is unwilling, or unable, to do the calculations necessary to translate small line drawings into usable quick-cut blocks. Block-pattern books are available, but in many of these the pattern for each block is given in just one size. The same is true of most block patterns published in quilting magazines.

This block book—a follow-up to *Around the Block*—is different. Designed for the quilter who loves both old patterns and modern rotary-cutting techniques, it provides clear, complete instructions in multiple sizes for each of 200 traditional and original blocks.

Brief how-to sections take you from quilt planning through borders, but the emphasis here is on blocks: a smorgasbord of popular patterns that you can quickly cut and piece in the size of your choice.

Using the Block Patterns

The block patterns appear in alphabetical order. Many blocks have more than one familiar name; a block you commonly refer to as Snail's Trail may be known by other quilters as Monkey Wrench or Indiana Puzzle. If you don't readily find the block you are looking for, it may appear under a different name. Sometimes one block may be identical to another block in the size, shape, and placement of its pieces, but because the arrangement of values (lights, mediums, and darks) is different, it will have a different name. Compare "Cross Roads" to "Texas" and "Kentucky Crossroads," for instance. The pieces are exactly the same, but the value arrangement is different, and each version has a unique name.

Block designs typically are drafted on regular, underlying grids. For example, a six-unit block is based on a grid that is six squares across and six down. In this book, a grid notation is included as part of each pattern.

Each block pattern includes a shaded drawing, a lettered drawing, both keyed to the cutting instructions; and a piecing diagram.

Most of the patterns produce a single block. For a few of the blocks, it is a more efficient use of fabric to cut the pieces two blocks at a time. Check each pattern to see how many blocks the instructions yield.

You can choose from one of six different finished sizes for each block. The finished sizes range from 4" to 14", depending on the particular block and the number of units it contains. You will find cutting instructions for the "standard" 12" block in many, but not all, of the patterns. Blocks based on five- and ten-unit grids simply do not translate well to a 12" format, as twelve is not divisible into quarters or eighths by either five or ten. It would be difficult to accurately measure and cut the 3.275" and 8.45" pieces that might be needed to make a 12" block from a design based on a five-unit grid.

We run into the same kind of measuring and cutting problems with the on-point squares and rectangles that are a feature of every block in this book. Templates are given for those shapes, so you can be sure your blocks will be accurately cut.

Making and Using Templates

Templates appear on pages 133–141. Trace any needed templates on paper or clear template plastic. Transfer all the information that is printed on the templates in the book to your paper or plastic templates, including the template numbers and the arrows that show grain lines. Carefully cut out the templates.

Accurate paper templates can be taped to the bottom of your cutting ruler with removable tape, giving you a guide for rotary cutting your shape. Or, place stiffened paper or plastic templates on your fabric, trace around them with a sharp pencil, and use scissors or your rotary cutter to cut on the traced lines.

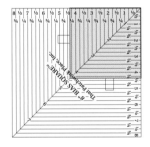

Paper template taped
to bottom of ruler

Cutting the Blocks

The block cutting directions are displayed in charts. These instructions are easy to follow once you are familiar with the terms and notations used throughout the book. Let's use the Boy's Nonsense pattern as an example. Note that the block is based on a three-unit grid, and that the cutting instructions produce one block.

Boy's Nonsense

3-Unit Grid

Color Illustration: page 11

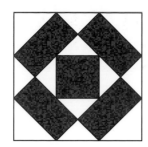 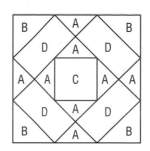 

FOR 1 BLOCK:			FINISHED BLOCK SIZE: *Single dimensions in the cutting chart indicate the size of the cut square (3" = 3" x 3")*					
			4½"	6"	7½"	9"	10½"	12"
Light	A: 2 ⊠→⊠		2¾"	3¼"	3¾"	4¼"	4¾"	5¼"
	B: 2 ◹→◹		2⅜"	2⅞"	3⅜"	3⅞"	4⅜"	4⅞"
Dark	C: 1 ☐		2"	2½"	3"	3½"	4"	4½"
	D: 4 ◇		T41	T51	T59	T67	T70	T72
Try this:	Reverse the lights and darks in every other block.							

The general instructions for this block call for a light fabric and a dark fabric. Refer to the shaded drawing to see where these values appear in the block. Some of the block patterns call for three values: light, medium, and dark. Others may require two different light fabrics (Light and Light 2) and/or two different medium fabrics (Medium and Medium 2) to define the pattern. When a pattern calls for two lights or two mediums, you could use two different prints of the same color, or two different colors of the same value.

Letters identify the various pattern pieces to cut. Check the lettered drawing to see where each of these pieces appears in the block.

In the cutting chart, a number and an icon follow each piece's letter designation. The number tells you how many pieces to cut, and the icon tells you what to cut. Six simple icons are used throughout the book:

☐ = Square(s)

◹→◹ = Square(s) cut once diagonally to make half-square triangles.

⊠→⊠ = Square(s) cut twice diagonally to make quarter-square triangles.

▭ = Rectangle(s)

◇ = On-point square(s); use template.

◇ = On-point rectangle(s); use template.

If the general cutting instruction says "A: 2 ☐," cut two squares. If the cutting instruction says "B: 4 ◹→◹," cut four squares, then cut the squares once diagonally to make the eight "Piece B" half-square triangles needed for the block. If the cutting instruction says "C: 1 ⊠→⊠," cut one square, then cut the square twice diagonally to make the four "Piece C" quarter-square triangles required. If the cutting instruction says "D: 2 ▭," cut two rectangles. If it says "E: 1 ◇," or "E: 1 ◇," you will need to make a template.

The cutting dimensions or template number for these pieces appear in the columns to the right of the general cutting instructions. For example, if you want to make a Boy's Nonsense block that finishes to 9", follow the general cutting instructions, using the dimensions given in the 9" Finished Block Size column:

▸ The first cutting instruction (A: 2 ⊠→⊠) tells you to cut two squares from the light fabric and to cut each square twice diagonally to make a total of eight quarter-square triangles. For a 9" block, cut 4¼" x 4¼" squares.

▸ The second cutting instruction (B:2 ◹→◹) tells you to cut two squares from the light fabric and to cut each square once diagonally to make a total of four half-square triangles. For a 9" block, cut 3⅞" x 3⅞" squares.

- The third cutting instruction (C: 1 ☐) tells you to cut one square from the dark fabric. For a 9" block, cut a 3½" x 3½" square.
- The final cutting instruction (D: 4 ◇) tells you to cut four on-point rectangles from the dark fabric. For a 9" block, use Template 67.

Both the templates and the rotary-cutting dimensions given include ¼"-wide seam allowances; *do not add seam allowances!*

Variations

Each block pattern includes a "Try this" notation that suggests a variation on the block. For the Boy's Nonsense block, I suggest reversing the lights and darks in every other block. This means that, for your second block, you would cut A and B from the dark fabric and C and D from the light.

Sometimes a "Try this" note will say something like "Use several different mediums for E." Increasing the number of fabrics used in the block while retaining the suggested value arrangement is a strategy worth considering for any of the block patterns. For the Boy's Nonsense block, for example, you could cut A from one light fabric and B from a different light. These could be two prints of the same color (or similar in color) but different in design scale or visual texture. Or, you could use two different colors, both light.

The "Try this" note for one block might well apply to several others. Read through the "Try this" notations throughout the book to get more ideas.

Many other variations are possible. Vary the contrast by combining lights and mediums or mediums and darks instead of lights and darks. Play with the value placement to create blocks with an entirely different look.

Rotary Cutting Individual Pieces

When cutting just a few pieces from a single fabric, use a small cutting ruler like the Bias Square®. If you want to cut several pieces at one time, fold or stack the fabric into as many as four layers. Place the Bias Square on one corner of the fabric, aligning the edges with the fabric grain (sometimes it is easier to see the grain from the wrong side of the fabric). If the fabric edges are uneven, make sure that the ruler markings for the dimensions you wish to cut do not extend beyond the fabric or overlap the selvage. For example, if you need a 3" square, make sure the 3" markings on the Bias Square are well within the fabric edges. Cut the first two sides. Rotate your cutting mat or turn the cut piece of fabric. Align the proper measurement on the Bias Square along the edges you just cut, and cut the opposite two sides.

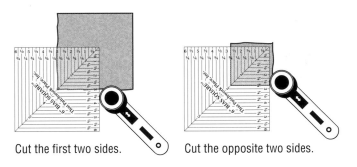

Cut the first two sides.   Cut the opposite two sides.

TIP: Often, when I need just one or two pieces from a particular fabric, I leave the fabric folded just as it comes from my shelf. I slide a small cutting mat between the layers and cut out the corner or a short strip without disturbing my careful folds.

Stitching Tips for Square-in-a-Square Units

1. Join the opposing triangles first, centering the triangles on the square. The triangle points will be sticking out about ⅜" beyond the edges of the square. Press seams toward the triangles.

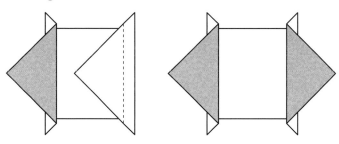

2. Join the remaining triangles. Your ¼" seam should exactly intersect the 90-degree angle where the two triangles meet at both the top and bottom ends of the seam, as in the magnified areas of the drawing. Adjust the position of the loose triangle until the seam lines up correctly at A. Take a few stitches, then adjust the points at B and finish stitching the seam. Press seams toward the triangles.

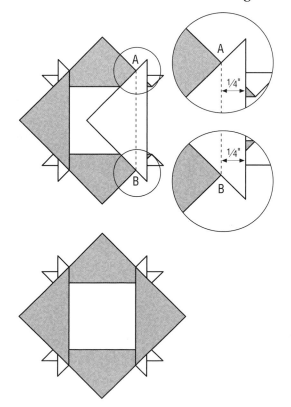

Stitching Tips for Flying Geese Units

1. Join the left-hand triangle: Match points (A) and bottom edges; sew in the direction of the arrow. Press seam toward the smaller triangle.

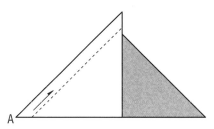

2. Join the right-hand triangle. Start at the arrow. Your ¼" seam should exactly intersect the 90-degree angle where the two smaller triangles meet, as in the magnified portion of the drawing. Adjust the position of the loose triangle until the seam lines up correctly. Take a few stitches, then match points (B) and finish stitching the seam. Press seam toward the smaller triangle.

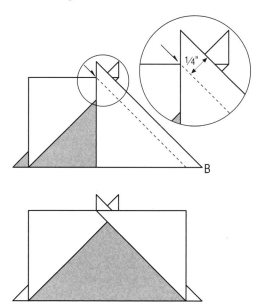

Planning Your Quilt

You almost certainly will want to use these patterns to make quilts, not just blocks. Some quilters plan their quilts before they begin making blocks; others construct a number of blocks before they decide how to set them together into a quilt. Whichever approach you take, there are numerous setting options to consider. Work with your blocks or with photocopies of a shaded block drawing. Try several different arrangements: side by side, side by side with every other block rotated, on point, with plain or pieced alternate blocks, or with plain or pieced sashing. Or consider a strippy arrangement, where horizontal or vertical bands of blocks are separated by plain or pieced bars. You'll find lots of ideas in *Sensational Settings: Over 80 Ways to Arrange Your Quilt Blocks* by Joan Hanson (That Patchwork Place).

While some quilts are planned so the pattern or design extends to the outside edges, most quilts have a patterned center section surrounded by borders. Decisions you make about the size, number, and layout of the blocks will determine the size of the patterned section of your quilt. The border width will establish the final dimensions. If you are making a quilt for the wall, the design and proportion of the piece are often more important than the size. Quilts for beds, on the other hand, must be made to a specific size.

Once I've chosen a setting arrangement, I sketch out a quilt plan on a work sheet like one of those provided on pages 131–132. This makes it easy for me to calculate the size of the patterned section of the quilt and to count the number of blocks and setting pieces I will need. For bed quilts, I plan the patterned section of the quilt, then select a border width that will bring the quilt to the desired finished dimensions. I work within general size guidelines that give me some room for design flexibility.

QUILT SIZE GUIDELINES

	Width	Length
Baby	36" – 45"	45" – 54"
Crib	42" – 48"	54" – 60"
Nap	54" – 60"	68" – 76"
Twin	56" – 64"	84" – 100"
Double	70" – 80"	84" – 100"
Queen	76" – 84"	90" – 104"
King	92" – 100"	90" – 104"

Making Multiple Blocks

When you use these block patterns to make a repeat-block quilt, you will not want to cut out the blocks one a time. Instead, multiply the numbers in the cutting-instruction column by the number of blocks you wish to make, and cut all the identical pieces at the same time. Before you do these calculations, check to see if the block pattern yields more than one block. The Boy's Nonsense pattern on page 00 produces one block. To make twenty Boy's Nonsense blocks, multiply the numbers in the cutting-instruction column by 20, and cut 40 A, 40 B, 20 C and 80 D. To make 20 blocks from a pattern that yields two blocks, multiply the numbers in the cutting-instruction column by ten, not twenty.

When cutting many identical pieces from a single fabric, common practice is to cut selvage-to-selvage strips to the proper width, then subcut the strips into squares or rectangles. For a refresher on basic rotary-cutting techniques, refer to *Shortcuts: A Concise Guide to Rotary Cutting* by Donna Lynn Thomas (That Patchwork Place).

Remember, it is always wise to make a sample block to test the pattern and confirm your fabric choices before cutting up yards of fabric!

When you make several blocks from a single pattern, watch for opportunities to use quick triangle-piecing techniques, strip-piecing methods, or other shortcuts from your own arsenal of tricks. A number of the blocks in this book contain four-patch units, for instance. Construct them with your favorite strip-piecing method instead of cutting and joining the individual squares.

Calculating Yardage Requirements

The first step in calculating yardage requirements for multiple blocks is to figure out how many of each shape you can get from a selvage-to-selvage strip cut to one of the shape's dimensions. Pattern writers commonly count on 42" of usable width from commercial fabrics. So if you need a total of forty 2" x 2" squares, first determine how many squares you can get from one 2" x 42" strip. Divide 42" by 2 to get 21.

Next, determine how many strips you will need. Divide the total number of squares needed (40) by the number of squares per strip (21) and round up to the next whole number to get 2.

Finally, multiply the cut width of the strips (2") by the number of strips needed (2) to get 4".

Do these calculations for each of the shapes, then add the results to find the total number of inches needed from each fabric. I usually add 3" to the total, to allow for fabric shrinkage and distortion, then divide the final figure by 36 to determine the total yardage required.

Let's calculate the total amount of light fabric needed for twenty 9" Boy's Nonsense blocks as an example (refer to the cutting instructions on page 35).

PIECE A:

For 20 blocks you need 40 squares,
    each 4¼" x 4¼".
One strip, 4¼" x 42", yields 9 squares
    (42 divided by 4.25 = 9.88).
You need 5 strips to get 40 squares (40 divided
    by 9 = 4.44; round up to 5).
So you need 21¼" of fabric for A (4.25" x 5).

PIECE B:

For 20 blocks you need 40 squares, each
    3⅞" x 3⅞".
One strip, 3⅞" x 42", yields 10 squares
    (42 divided by 3.875 = 10.84).
You need 4 strips to get 40 squares (40 divided
    by 10 = 4).
So you need 15½" of fabric for B (3.875" x 4).

The total yardage needed for pieces A and B is 36¾". Adding 3" to allow for distortion and shrinkage brings the final figure to 39¾", or about 1⅛ yards of a light fabric.

DECIMAL-TO-INCH CONVERSIONS		
.0625	=	¹⁄₁₆"
.125	=	⅛"
.1875	=	³⁄₁₆"
.25	=	¼"
.3125	=	⁵⁄₁₆"
.375	=	⅜"
.4375	=	⁷⁄₁₆"
.5	=	½"
.5625	=	⁹⁄₁₆"
.625	=	⅝"
.6875	=	¹¹⁄₁₆"
.75	=	¾"
.8125	=	¹³⁄₁₆"
.875	=	⅞"
.9375	=	¹⁵⁄₁₆"

Gallery of Blocks

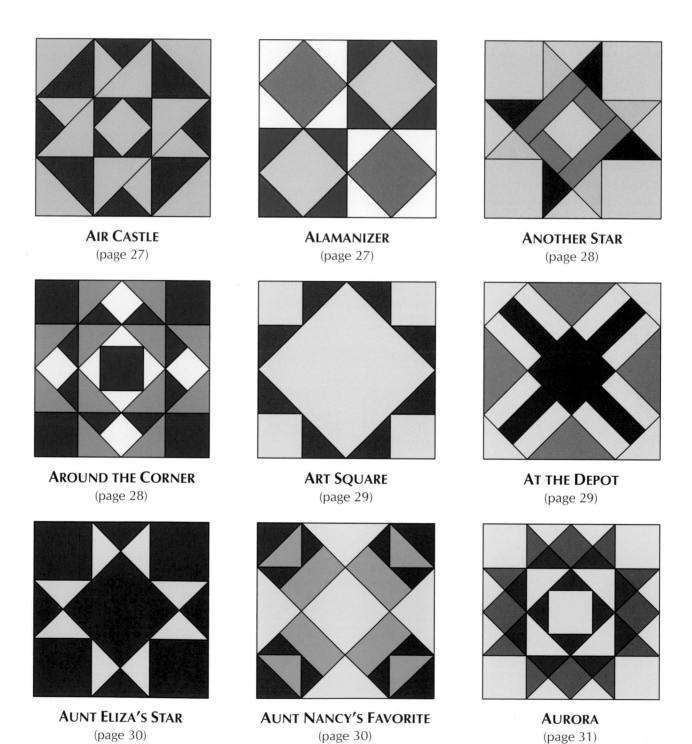

AIR CASTLE
(page 27)

ALAMANIZER
(page 27)

ANOTHER STAR
(page 28)

AROUND THE CORNER
(page 28)

ART SQUARE
(page 29)

AT THE DEPOT
(page 29)

AUNT ELIZA'S STAR
(page 30)

AUNT NANCY'S FAVORITE
(page 30)

AURORA
(page 31)

BALTIMORE BELLE
(page 31)

BASEMENT WINDOW
(page 32)

BEACON LIGHTS
(page 32)

BEAVER POND
(page 33)

BIRD'S NEST
(page 33)

BLYTHE'S BEST
(page 34)

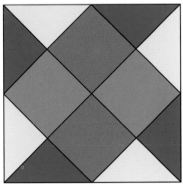

BOXES
(page 34)

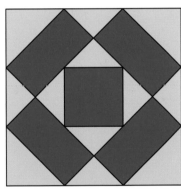

BOY'S NONSENSE
(page 35)

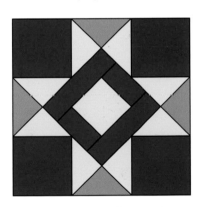

BRACED STAR
(page 35)

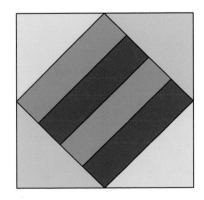

BREAKUP
(page 36)

BROKEN IRISH CHAIN
(page 37)

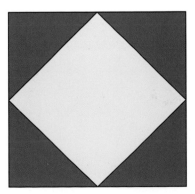

BROKEN SASH
(page 37)

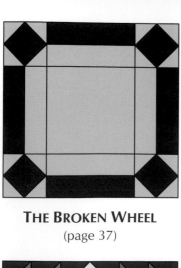

THE BROKEN WHEEL
(page 37)

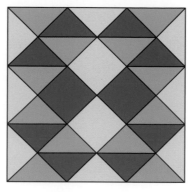

BUCKWHEAT
(page 38)

CARD BASKET
(page 38)

CAROL'S SCRAP TIME QUILT
(page 39)

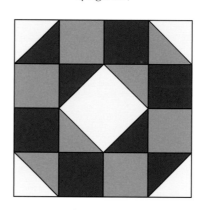

CASTLES IN SPAIN
(page 39)

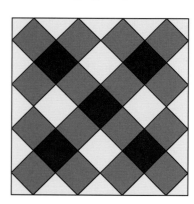

CATS AND MICE
(page 40)

CENTENNIAL
(page 40)

CHEYENNE
(page 41)

CHICAGO PAVEMENTS
(page 41)

CHILKOOT TRAIL
(page 42)

CHINOOK
(page 42)

CHRISTMAS STAR
(page 43)

12

CHUCK A LUCK
(page 43)

COBBLESTONES
(page 44)

COCK'S COMB
(page 44)

COFFIN STAR
(page 45)

THE COG BLOCK
(page 45)

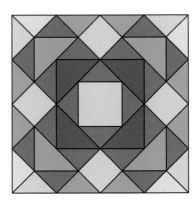

COLONIAL GARDEN
(page 46)

COMBINATION STAR
(page 46)

CONNECTICUT
(page 47)

CORNER STAR
(page 47)

COUNTRY CHECKERS
(page 48)

COUNTY FAIR
(page 48)

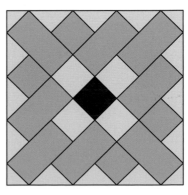

COURTHOUSE LAWN
(page 49)

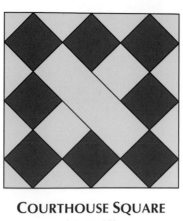

COURTHOUSE SQUARE
(page 49)

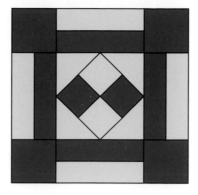

COXEY'S CAMP
(page 50)

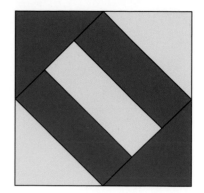

CRACKER
(page 50)

CROSS AND CHAINS
(page 51)

CROSS ROADS
(page 51)

CROSS ROADS TO JERICHO
(page 52)

CROSS ROADS TO TEXAS
(page 52)

CROSSED SQUARES
(page 53)

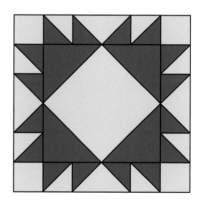

CROWN
(page 53)

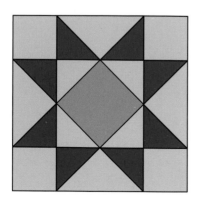

CRYSTAL STAR
(page 54)

DARIEN'S DILEMMA
(page 54)

DENALI
(page 55)

A DESIGN FOR PATRIOTISM
(page 55)

DEVIL'S CLAWS II
(page 56)

DOMINO AND SQUARE
(page 56)

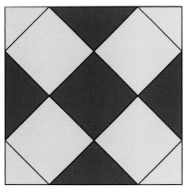

DOUBLE CROSS
(page 57)

THE DOUBLE SQUARE
(page 57)

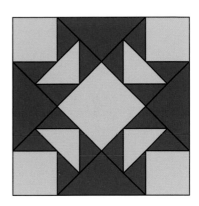

DOUBLE T
(page 58)

EAGLE'S NEST
(page 58)

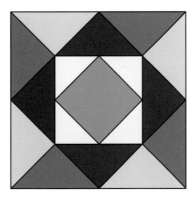

ECONOMY
(page 59)

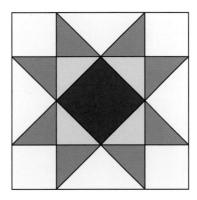

EIGHT POINTED STAR
(page 59)

EVA'S DELIGHT
(page 60)

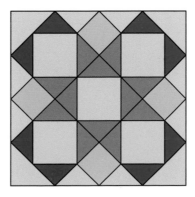

FEDERAL SQUARE
(page 60)

FIVE CROSSES
(page 61)

15

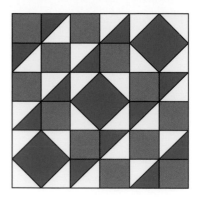

FIVE DIAMONDS
(page 61)

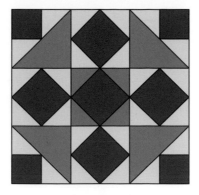

FIVE SPOT
(page 62)

FLYING SHUTTLES
(page 62)

FOUR SQUARES
(page 63)

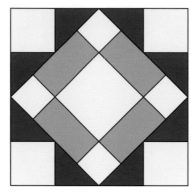

FOUR-FOUR TIME
(page 63)

FOX PAWS
(page 64)

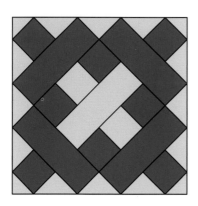

FRIENDSHIP CHAIN
(page 64)

THE FRIENDSHIP QUILT
(page 65)

FRIENDSHIP QUILT II
(page 65)

GARDEN OF EDEN
(page 66)

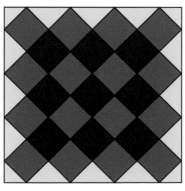

THE GARDEN PATCH
(page 66)

GEM BLOCK
(page 67)

GEORGETOWN CIRCLE
(page 67)

GLACIER BAY
(page 68)

GOLD RUSH
(page 68)

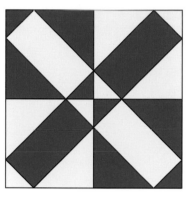

GOOD FORTUNE
(page 69)

GOOSE IN THE POND
(page 69)

GRANDMOTHER'S CROSS
(page 70)

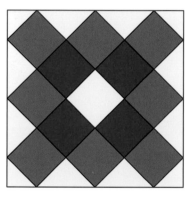

GRANDMOTHER'S PRIDE
(page 70)

GRECIAN SQUARE II
(page 71)

THE H SQUARE QUILT
(page 71)

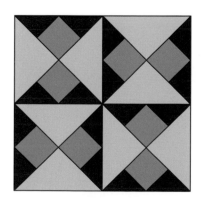

HAZY DAISY
(page 72)

HILL AND CRAG
(page 72)

HITHER AND YON
(page 73)

HOME CIRCLE
(page 73)

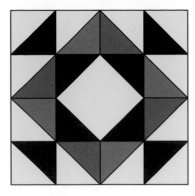

HOUR GLASS II
(page 74)

THE HOUSE JACK BUILT
(page 74)

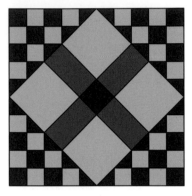

IDITAROD TRAIL
(page 75)

ILLINOIS
(page 75)

IMPERIAL T
(page 76)

IMPROVED FOUR PATCH
(page 76)

INDIAN MAZE
(page 77)

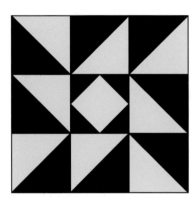

INDIANA PUZZLE
(page 77)

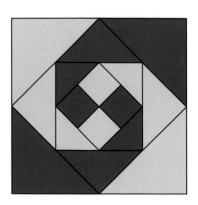

INDIANA PUZZLE II
(page 78)

INSIDE PASSAGE
(page 78)

IRISH CHAIN
(page 79)

18

JACK IN THE PULPIT
(page 79)

JACK'S DELIGHT
(page 80)

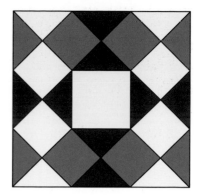

JEFFERSON CITY
(page 80)

JOSEPH'S COAT
(page 81)

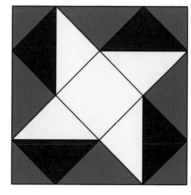

JULY FOURTH
(page 81)

JUNEAU
(page 82)

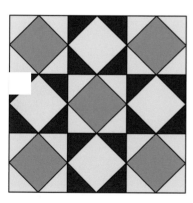

KANSAS STAR
(page 82)

KENTUCKY CROSSROADS
(page 83)

LADIES' AID BLOCK
(page 83)

LINCOLN
(page 84)

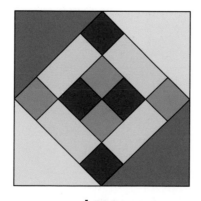

LOLA
(page 84)

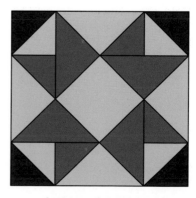

MAGIC CROSS
(page 85)

MALVINA'S CHAIN
(page 85)

MEMORY BLOCKS II
(page 86)

MIDNIGHT SUN
(page 86)

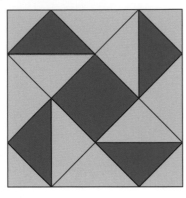

MILL WHEEL
(page 87)

MINERAL WELLS
(page 87)

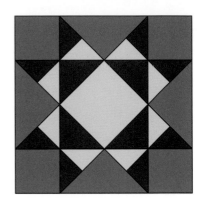

MISSOURI STAR
(page 88)

MOSAIC
(page 88)

MOSAIC #3
(page 89)

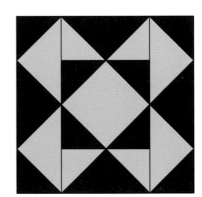

MOSAIC #10
(page 89)

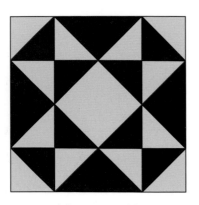

MOSAIC #19
(page 90)

MOSAIC #21
(page 90)

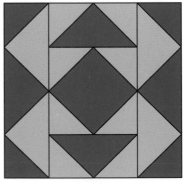

MOSAIC #22
(page 91)

MOSAIC ROSE
(page 91)

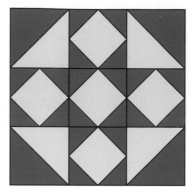

MRS. BROWN'S CHOICE
(page 92)

NEW ALBUM
(page 92)

NEW HAMPSHIRE'S GRANITE ROCK
(page 93)

NEW HOUR GLASS
(page 93)

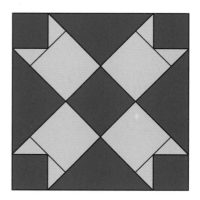

NINE PATCH CHECKERBOARD
(page 94)

NORTHUMBERLAND STAR
(page 94)

ODD FELLOWS
(page 95)

ODD FELLOW'S CROSS
(page 95)

THE OLD RUGGED CROSS
(page 96)

OLD TIME BLOCK
(page 96)

AN ORIGINAL DESIGN
(page 97)

21

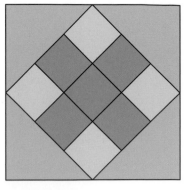

PATTERN WITHOUT A NAME
(page 97)

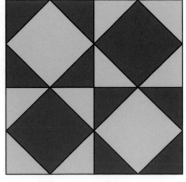

PAVEMENT PATTERN
(page 98)

PERSHING
(page 98)

PYRAMIDS
(page 99)

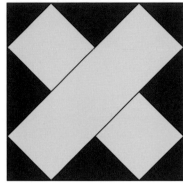

QUILT IN LIGHT AND DARK
(page 99)

RED CROSS
(page 100)

REVERSE X
(page 100)

RHODE ISLAND
(page 101)

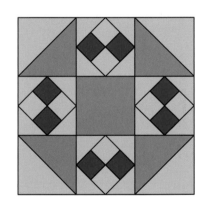

RICHMOND
(page 101)

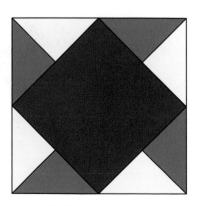

RIGHT AND LEFT
(page 102)

ROCKY GLEN II
(page 102)

ROCKY MOUNTAIN CHAIN
(page 103)

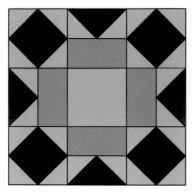

ROLLING SQUARES
(page 103)

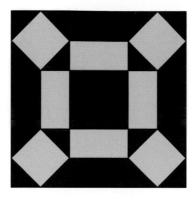

ROLLING STONE
(page 104)

ROMAN CROSS
(page 104)

ST. JOHN PAVEMENT
(page 105)

SALLY'S FAVORITE
(page 105)

SALT LAKE CITY
(page 106)

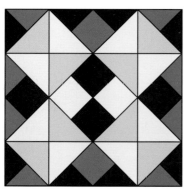

A SALUTE TO THE COLORS
(page 106)

SCOTCH SQUARES
(page 107)

SNAIL'S TRAIL II
(page 107)

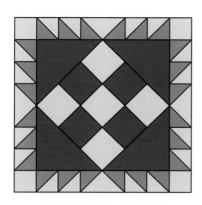

SPRING HAS COME
(page 108)

THE SQUARE DEAL
(page 108)

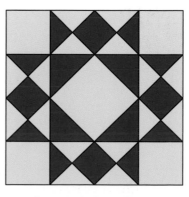

SQUARE AND STAR
(page 109)

SQUIRREL IN A CAGE
(page 109)

THE STAR AND BLOCK
(page 110)

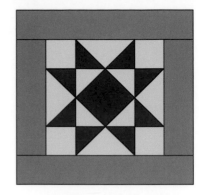

STAR OF VIRGINIA
(page 110)

STAR X
(page 111)

STORM SIGNAL
(page 111)

SUNSHINE
(page 112)

T SQUARE
(page 112)

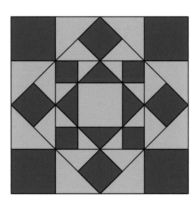

TEMPLE COURT
(page 113)

THUNDER AND LIGHTNING
(page 113)

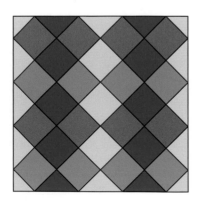

TINTED CHAINS
(page 114)

TOAD IN A PUDDLE
(page 114)

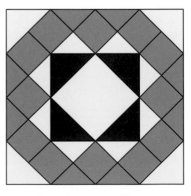

TOMBSTONE QUILT
(page 115)

TOTEM
(page 115)

TRACY'S PUZZLE
(page 116)

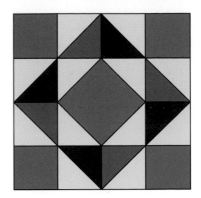

TRIANGLE SQUARES
(page 116)

TRIANGLES
(page 117)

TURKEY IN THE STRAW
(page 117)

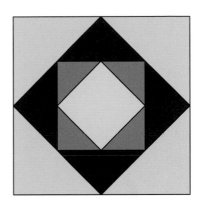

TWELVE TRIANGLES
(page 118)

UNION SQUARE
(page 118)

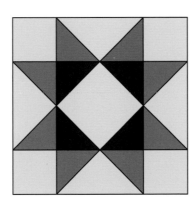

VARIABLE STAR
(page 119)

VIRGINA REEL
(page 119)

WASHINGTON PAVEMENT
(page 120)

THE WEDDING RING
(page 120)

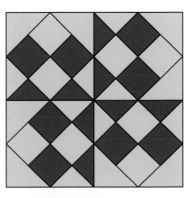

WHIRLING SQUARES
(page 121)

WHIRLWIND
(page 121)

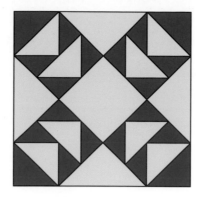

WILD GOOSE
(page 122)

WILD GOOSE CHASE II
(page 122)

WILD GOOSE CHASE III
(page 123)

WILLOW HAVEN
(page 123)

WINDBLOWN SQUARE
(page 124)

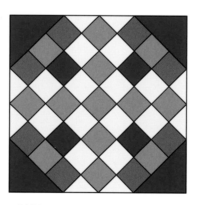

WINDOWS AND DOORS
(page 124)

WOODLAND PATH
(page 125)

THE X
(page 125)

YELLOW CLOVER
(page 126)

ZENOBIA'S PUZZLE
(page 126)

Block Patterns

Air Castle

6-Unit Grid

Color Illustration: page 10

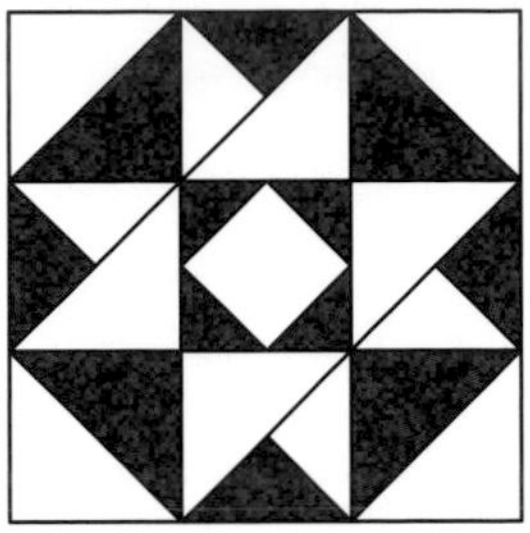
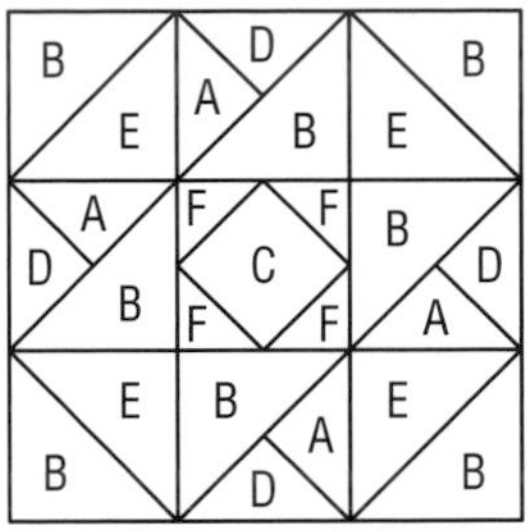

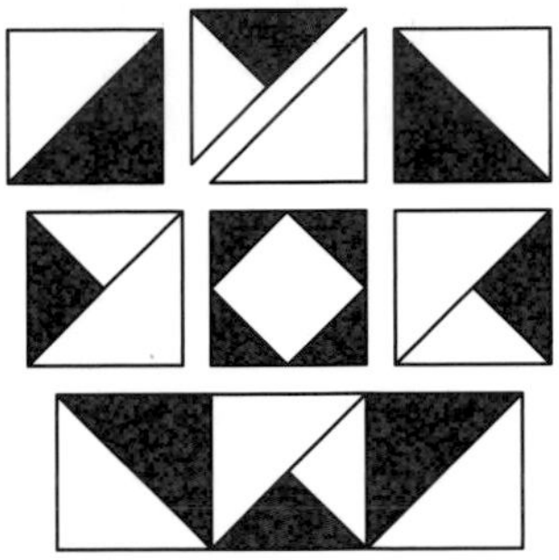

FOR 1 BLOCK:

FINISHED BLOCK SIZE: *Single dimensions in the cutting chart indicate the size of the cut square (3" = 3" x 3")*

		4½"	6"	7½"	9"	10½"	12"
Light	A: 1	2¾"	3¼"	3¾"	4¼"	4¾"	5¼"
	B: 4	2⅜"	2⅞"	3⅜"	3⅞"	4⅜"	4⅞"
	C: 1	T5	T7	T9	T11	T12	T14
Dark	D: 1	2¾"	3¼"	3¾"	4¼"	4¾"	5¼"
	E: 2	2⅜"	2⅞"	3⅜"	3⅞"	4⅜"	4⅞
	F: 2	1⅝"	1⅞"	2⅛"	2⅜"	2⅝"	2⅞"
Try this:	Use one light for A and C and a different light for B.						

Alamanizer

4-Unit Grid

Color Illustration: page 10

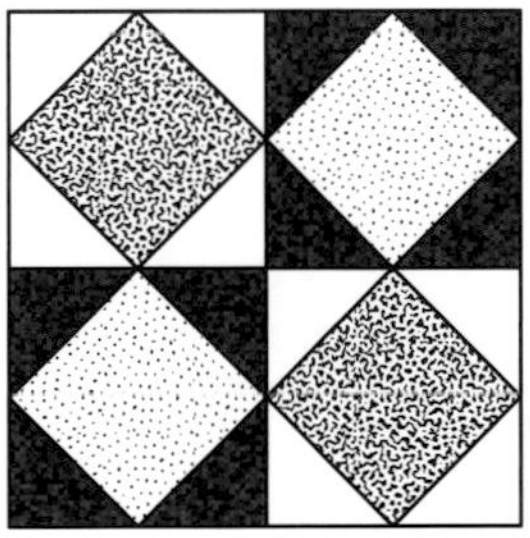
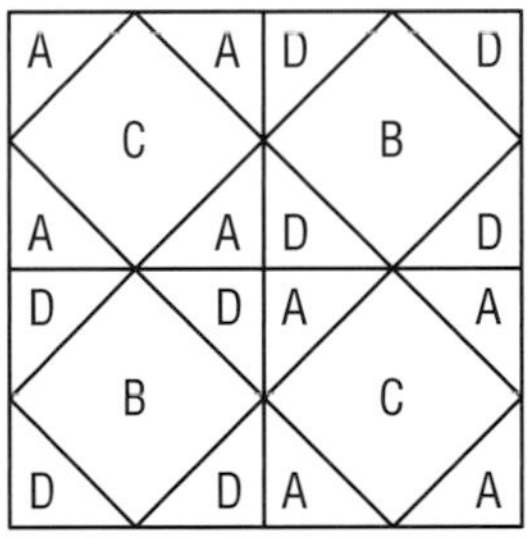

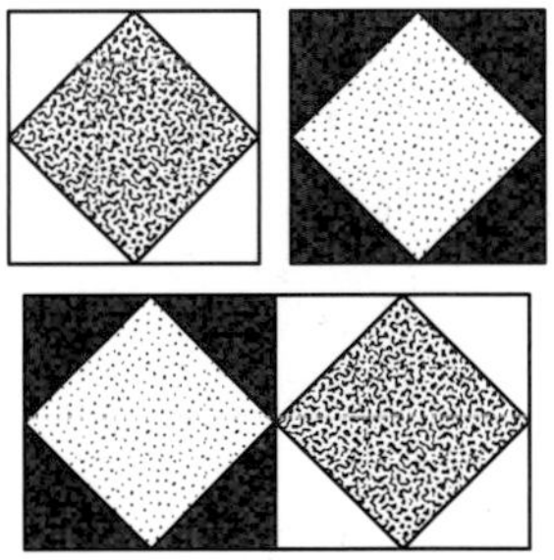

FOR 1 BLOCK:

FINISHED BLOCK SIZE: *Single dimensions in the cutting chart indicate the size of the cut square (3" = 3" x 3")*

		4"	6"	8"	9"	10"	12"
Light	A: 4	1⅞"	2⅜"	2⅞"	3⅛"	3⅜"	3⅞"
Light 2	B: 2	T7	T11	T14	T15	T16	T19
Medium	C: 2	T7	T11	T14	T15	T16	T19
Dark	D: 4	1⅞"	2⅜"	2⅞"	3⅛"	3⅜"	3⅞"
Try this:	Use several different fabrics for B and C.						

Another Star

6-Unit Grid

Color Illustration: page 10

 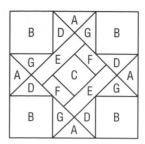 

		FINISHED BLOCK SIZE: *Single dimensions in the cutting chart indicate the size of the cut square (3" = 3" x 3")*					
FOR 1 BLOCK:		**4½"**	**6"**	**7½"**	**9"**	**10½"**	**12"**
Light	A: 1 ⊠→⊠	2¾"	3¼"	3¾"	4¼"	4¾"	5¼"
	B: 4 ☐	2"	2½"	3"	3½"	4"	4½"
	C: 1 ◇	T5	T7	T9	T11	T12	T14
Light 2	D: 1 ⊠→⊠	2¾"	3¼"	3¾"	4¼"	4¾"	5¼"
Medium	E: 2 ◇	T30	T34	T38	T43	T48	T53
	F: 2 ◇	T28	T32	T36	T41	T46	T51
Dark	G: 1 ⊠→⊠	2¾"	3¼"	3¾"	4¼"	4¾"	5¼"
Try this:		Use the dark fabric for all the star points (D and G).					

Around the Corner

4-Unit Grid

Color Illustration: page 10

 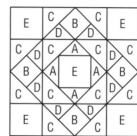 

		FINISHED BLOCK SIZE: *Single dimensions in the cutting chart indicate the size of the cut square (3" = 3" x 3")*					
FOR 1 BLOCK:		**4"**	**6"**	**8"**	**9"**	**10"**	**12"**
Light	A: 1 ⊠→⊠	2¼"	2¾"	3¼"	3½"	3¾"	4¼"
	B: 4 ◇	T2	T5	T7	T8	T9	T11
Medium	C: 6 ☐→◻	1⅞"	2⅜"	2⅞"	3⅛"	3⅜"	3⅞"
Dark	D: 2 ⊠→⊠	2¼"	2¾"	3¼"	3½"	3¾"	4¼"
	E: 5 ☐	1½"	2"	2½"	2¾"	3"	3½"
Try this:		Reverse the mediums and darks in every other block.					

☐ *Light*   ░ *Light 2*   ▒ *Medium*   ▓ *Medium 2*   ■ *Dark*

Art Square

4-Unit Grid
Color Illustration: page 10

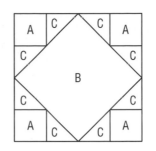
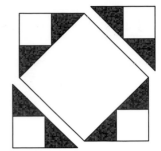

FOR 1 BLOCK:			FINISHED BLOCK SIZE: *Single dimensions in the cutting chart indicate the size of the cut square (3" = 3" x 3")*					
			4"	**6"**	**8"**	**9"**	**10"**	**12"**
Light	A: 4	⬜	1½"	2"	2½"	2¾"	3"	3½"
	B: 1	◇	T14	T19	T23	T24	T25	T27
Dark	C: 4	◿▶◺	1⅞"	2⅜"	2⅞"	3⅛"	3⅜"	3⅞"
Try this:		Use a large-scale print for B.						

At the Depot

6-Unit Grid
Color Illustration: page 10

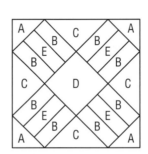

FOR 1 BLOCK:			FINISHED BLOCK SIZE: *Single dimensions in the cutting chart indicate the size of the cut square (3" = 3" x 3")*					
			4½"	**6"**	**7½"**	**9"**	**10½"**	**12"**
Light	A: 2	◿▶◺	2"	2⅜"	2¾"	3⅛"	3½"	3⅞"
	B: 8	◇	T29	T33	T37	T42	T47	T52
Medium	C: 1	⊠▶⊠	3½"	4¼"	5"	5¾"	6½"	7¼"
Dark	D: 1	◇	T8	T11	T13	T15	T17	T19
	E: 4	◇	T29	T33	T37	T42	T47	T52
Try this:		Use a medium instead of a light for A.						

Aunt Eliza's Star

3-Unit Grid

Color Illustration: page 10

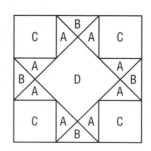

FOR 1 BLOCK:			FINISHED BLOCK SIZE: *Single dimensions in the cutting chart indicate the size of the cut square (3" = 3" x 3")*					
			4½"	6"	7½"	9"	10½"	12"
Light	A: 2 ⊠→⊠		2¾"	3¼"	3¾"	4¼"	4¾"	5¼"
Dark	B: 1 ⊠→⊠		2¾"	3¼"	3¾"	4¼"	4¾"	5¼
	C: 4 ☐		2"	2½"	3"	3½"	4"	4½"
	D: 1 ◇		T11	T14	T16	T19	T21	T23
Try this:	Reverse the lights and darks in every other block.							

Aunt Nancy's Favorite

4-Unit Grid

Color Illustration: page 10

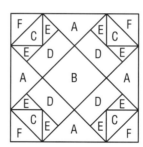

FOR 1 BLOCK:			FINISHED BLOCK SIZE: *Single dimensions in the cutting chart indicate the size of the cut square (3" = 3" x 3")*					
			4"	6"	8"	9"	10"	12"
Light	A: 1 ⊠→⊠		3¼"	4¼"	5¼"	5¾"	6¼"	7¼"
	B: 1 ◇		T7	T11	T14	T15	T16	T19
Medium	C: 2 ☐→◱		1⅞"	2⅜"	2⅞"	3⅛"	3⅜"	3⅞"
	D: 4 ◇		T32	T41	T51	T56	T59	T67
Dark	E: 2 ⊠→⊠		2¼"	2¾"	3¼"	3½"	3¾"	4¼"
	F: 2 ◳→◰		1⅞"	2⅜"	2⅞"	3⅛"	3⅜"	3⅞"
Try this:	Use one medium for C and a different medium for D.							

☐ *Light* ░ *Light 2* ▦ *Medium* ▩ *Medium 2* ■ *Dark*

Aurora

4-Unit Grid

Color Illustration: page 10

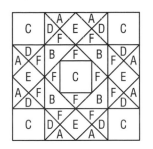

		FINISHED BLOCK SIZE: *Single dimensions in the cutting chart indicate the size of the cut square (3" = 3" x 3")*					
FOR 1 BLOCK:		**4"**	**6"**	**8"**	**9"**	**10"**	**12**
Light	A: 2 ⊠→⊠	2¼"	2¾"	3¼"	3½"	3¾"	4¼"
	B: 2 ◻→⊠	1⅞"	2⅜"	2⅞"	3⅛"	3⅜"	3⅞"
	C: 5 ◻	1½"	2"	2½"	2¾"	3"	3½"
Medium	D: 2 ⊠→⊠	2¼"	2¾"	3¼"	3½"	3¾"	4¼"
	E: 4 ◇	T2	T5	T7	T8	T9	T11
Dark	F: 3 ⊠→⊠	2¼"	2¾"	3¼"	3½"	3¾"	4¼"

Try this: Use one medium for D and a different medium for E.

NOTE: *This block is listed as "Nameless" in Barbara Brackman's* Encyclopedia of Pieced Quilt Patterns; *the source given is Clara Stone's* Practical Needlework: Quilt Patterns *booklet, published in 1906. For this book, I've chosen to call the block "Aurora."*

Baltimore Belle

6-Unit Grid

Color Illustration: page 11

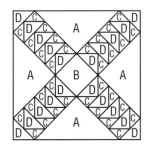

		FINISHED BLOCK SIZE: *Single dimensions in the cutting chart indicate the size of the cut square (3" = 3" x 3")*					
FOR 1 BLOCK:		**4½"**	**6"**	**7½"**	**9"**	**10½"**	**12"**
Light	A: 1 ⊠→⊠	4¼"	5¼"	6¼"	7¼"	8¼"	9¼"
	B: 1 ◇	T5	T7	T9	T11	T12	T14
Medium	C: 8 ⊠→⊠	2"	2¼"	2½"	2¾"	3"	3¼"
Dark	D: 10 ◻→⊠	1⅝"	1⅞"	2⅛"	2⅜"	2⅝"	2⅞"

Try this: Use many different mediums for C.

Basement Window

8-Unit Grid

Color Illustration: page 11

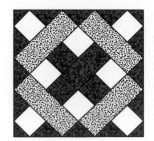 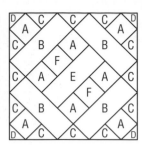 

				FINISHED BLOCK SIZE: *Single dimensions in the cutting chart indicate the size of the cut square (3" = 3" x 3")*				
FOR 1 BLOCK:			**6"**	**8"**	**9"**	**10"**	**12"**	**14"**
Light	A: 8 ◇		T5	T7	T8	T9	T11	T12
Medium	B: 4 ◇		T42	T52	T57	T60	T68	T71
Dark	C: 3 ⊠→⊠		2¾"	3¼"	3½"	3¾"	4¼"	4¾"
	D: 2 ◻→⊠		1⅝"	1⅞"	2"	2⅛"	2⅜"	2⅝"
	E: 1 ◇		T42	T52	T57	T60	T68	T71
	F: 2 ◇		T5	T7	T8	T9	T11	T12
Try this:	Reverse the lights and darks in every other block.							

Beacon Lights

4-Unit Grid

Color Illustration: page 11

 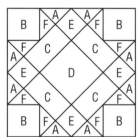 

				FINISHED BLOCK SIZE: *Single dimensions in the cutting chart indicate the size of the cut square (3" = 3" x 3")*				
FOR 1 BLOCK:			**4"**	**6"**	**8"**	**9"**	**10"**	**12"**
Light	A: 2 ⊠→⊠		2¼"	2¾"	3¼"	3½"	3¾"	4¼"
	B: 4 ◻		1½"	2"	2½"	2¾"	3"	3½"
	C: 4 ◇		T32	T41	T51	T56	T59	T67
Medium	D: 1 ◇		T7	T11	T14	T15	T16	T19
	E: 4 ◇		T2	T5	T7	T8	T9	T11
Dark	F: 2 ⊠→⊠		2¼"	2¾"	3¼"	3½"	3¾"	4¼"
Try this:	Use one light for A and B and a different light for C.							

◻ Light   ▦ Light 2   ▨ Medium   ▩ Medium 2   ■ Dark

Beaver Pond

2-Unit Grid

Color Illustration: page 11

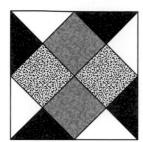 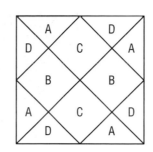 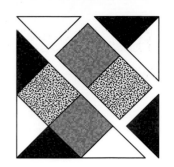

FOR 1 BLOCK:		FINISHED BLOCK SIZE *Single dimensions in the cutting chart indicate the size of the cut square (3" = 3" x 3")*					
		4"	**6"**	**8"**	**9"**	**10"**	**12"**
Light	A: 1	3¼"	4¼"	5¼"	5¾"	6¼"	7¼"
Medium	B: 2	T7	T11	T14	T15	T16	T19
Medium 2	C: 2	T7	T11	T14	T15	T16	T19
Dark	D: 1	3¼"	4¼"	5¼"	5¾"	6¼"	7¼"
Try this:		Use several different fabrics for B and C.					

Bird's Nest

10-Unit Grid

Color Illustration: page 11

 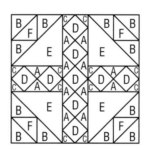  

FOR 1 BLOCK:		FINISHED BLOCK SIZE: *Single dimensions in the cutting chart indicate the size of the cut square (3" = 3" x 3")*					
		6¼"	**7½"**	**8¾"**	**10"**	**12½"**	**13¾"**
Light	A: 3	2½"	2¾"	3"	3¼"	3¾"	4"
	B: 6	2⅛"	2⅜"	2⅝"	2⅞"	3⅜"	3⅝"
	C: 6	1½"	1⅝"	1¾"	1⅞"	2⅛"	2¼"
Medium	D: 9	T4	T5	T6	T7	T9	T10
Dark	E: 2	3⅜"	3⅞"	4⅜"	4⅞"	5⅞"	6⅜"
	F: 2	2⅛"	2⅜"	2⅝"	2⅞"	3⅜"	3⅝"
Try this:		Use several different mediums for D.					

33

Blythe's Best

8-Unit Grid

Color Illustration: page 11

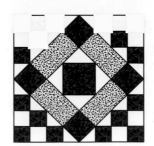
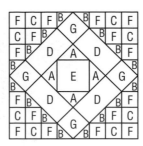

FOR 1 BLOCK:			FINISHED BLOCK SIZE: *Single dimensions in the cutting chart indicate the size of the cut square (3" = 3" x 3")*					
			6"	8"	9"	10"	12"	14"
Light	A: 1	⊠→⊠	2¾"	3¼"	3½"	3¾"	4¼"	4¾"
	B: 8	◺→◺	1⅝"	1⅞"	2"	2⅛"	2⅜"	2⅝"
	C: 8	▢	1¼"	1½"	1⅝"	1¾"	2"	2¼"
Medium	D: 4	◇	T41	T51	T56	T59	T67	T70
Dark	E: 1	▢	2"	2½"	2¾"	3"	3½"	4"
	F: 16	▢	1¼"	1½"	1⅝"	1¾"	2"	2¼"
	G: 4	◇	T5	T7	T8	T9	T11	T12
Try this:		Use one light for A and a different light for B and C.						

Boxes

6-Unit Grid

Color Illustration: page 11

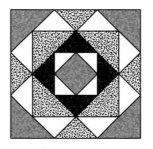
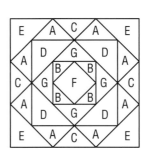

FOR 1 BLOCK:			FINISHED BLOCK SIZE: *Single dimensions in the cutting chart indicate the size of the cut square (3" = 3" x 3")*					
			4½"	6"	7½"	9"	10½"	12"
Light	A: 2	⊠→⊠	2¾"	3¼"	3¾"	4¼"	4¾"	5¼"
	B: 2	◺→◺	1⅝"	1⅞"	2⅛"	2⅜"	2⅝"	2⅞"
Medium	C: 1	⊠→⊠	2¾"	3¼"	3¾"	4¼"	4¾"	5¼"
	D: 2	◺→◺	2⅜"	2⅞"	3⅜"	3⅞"	4⅜"	4⅞"
Medium 2	E: 2	◺→◺	2⅜"	2⅞"	3⅜"	3⅞"	4⅜"	4⅞"
	F: 1	◇	T5	T7	T9	T11	T12	T14
Dark	G: 1	⊠→⊠	2¾"	3¼"	3¾"	4¼"	4¾"	5¼"
Try this:		Use a dark instead of a medium for E.						

▢ Light · ▦ Light 2 · ▨ Medium · ▩ Medium 2 · ■ Dark

Boy's Nonsense

3-Unit Grid

Color Illustration: page 11

 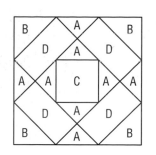 

FOR 1 BLOCK:			FINISHED BLOCK SIZE: *Single dimensions in the cutting chart indicate the size of the cut square (3" = 3" x 3")*					
			4½"	6"	7½"	9"	10½"	12"
Light	A: 2		2¾"	3¼"	3¾"	4¼"	4¾"	5¼"
	B: 2		2⅜"	2⅞"	3⅜"	3⅞"	4⅜"	4⅞"
Dark	C: 1		2"	2½"	3"	3½"	4"	4½"
	D: 4		T41	T51	T59	T67	T70	T72
Try this:		Reverse the lights and darks in every other block.						

Braced Star

6-Unit Grid

Color Illustration: page 11

 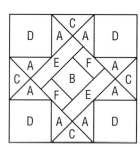 

FOR 1 BLOCK:			FINISHED BLOCK SIZE: *Single dimensions in the cutting chart indicate the size of the cut square (3" = 3" x 3")*					
			4½"	6"	7½"	9"	10½"	12"
Light	A: 2		2¾"	3¼"	3¾"	4¼"	4¾"	5¼"
	B: 1		T5	T7	T9	T11	T12	T14
Medium	C: 1		2¾"	3¼"	3¾"	4¼"	4¾"	5¼"
Dark	D: 4		2"	2½"	3"	3½"	4"	4½"
	E: 2		T30	T34	T38	T43	T48	T53
	F: 2		T28	T32	T36	T41	T46	T51
Try this:		Use a medium instead of a light for B.						

Breakup

4-Unit Grid

Color Illustration: page 11

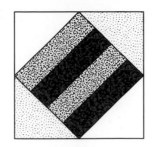
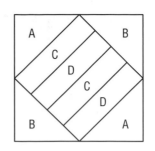
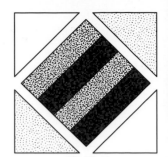

FOR 1 BLOCK:			FINISHED BLOCK SIZE: *Single dimensions in the cutting chart indicate the size of the cut square (3" = 3" x 3")*					
			4"	**6"**	**8"**	**9"**	**10"**	**12"**
Light	A: 1		2⅞"	3⅞"	4⅞"	5⅜"	5⅞"	6⅞"
Light 2	B: 1		2⅞"	3⅞"	4⅞"	5⅜"	5⅞"	6⅞"
Medium	C: 2		T34	T43	T53	T58	T61	T69
Dark	D: 2		T34	T43	T53	T58	T61	T69
Try this:		Use several different fabrics for C and D.						

Broken Irish Chain

5-Unit Grid

Color Illustration: page 11

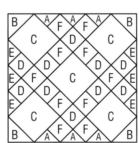

FOR 2 BLOCKS:			FINISHED BLOCK SIZE: *Single dimensions in the cutting chart indicate the size of the cut square (3" = 3" x 3")*					
			5"	**6¼"**	**7½"**	**8¾"**	**10"**	**12½"**
Light	A: 3		2¼"	2½"	2¾"	3"	3¼"	3¾"
	B: 4		1⅞"	2⅛"	2⅜"	2⅝"	2⅞"	3⅜"
	C: 10		T7	T9	T11	T12	T14	T16
	D: 20		T2	T4	T5	T6	T7	T9
Dark	E: 3		2¼"	2½"	2¾"	3"	3¼"	3¾"
	F: 20		T2	T4	T5	T6	T7	T9
Try this:		Use one light for A, B, and D, and a different light for C.						

☐ Light   ▧ Light 2   ▨ Medium   ▨ Medium 2   ■ Dark

Broken Sash

2-Unit Grid

Color Illustration: page 11

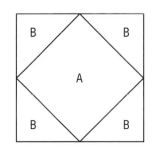
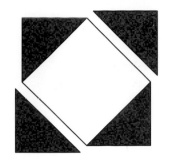

		FINISHED BLOCK SIZE					
		Single dimensions in the cutting chart indicate the size of the cut square (3" = 3" x 3")					
FOR 1 BLOCK:		**4"**	**6"**	**8"**	**9"**	**10"**	**12"**
Light	A: 1 ◇	T14	T19	T23	T24	T25	T27
Dark	B: 2 ◺→◹	2⅞"	3⅞"	4⅞"	5⅜"	5⅞"	6⅞"
Try this:		Use a large-scale print for A.					

The Broken Wheel

8-Unit Grid

Color Illustration: page 12

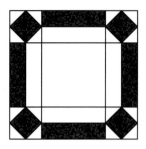
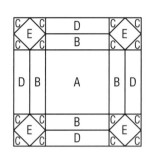
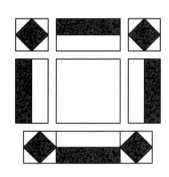

		FINISHED BLOCK SIZE:					
		Single dimensions in the cutting chart indicate the size of the cut square (3" = 3" x 3")					
FOR 1 BLOCK:		**6"**	**8"**	**9"**	**10"**	**12"**	**14"**
Light	A: 1 ☐	3½"	4½"	5"	5½"	6½"	7½"
	B: 4 ▭	1¼" x 3½"	1½" x 4½"	1⅝" x 5"	1¾" x 5½"	2" x 6½"	2¼" x 7½"
	C: 8 ◺→◹	1⅝"	1⅞"	2"	2⅛"	2⅜"	2⅝"
Dark	D: 4 ▭	1¼" x 3½"	1½" x 4½"	1⅝" x 5"	1¾" x 5½"	2" x 6½"	2¼" x 7½"
	E: 4 ◇	T5	T7	T8	T9	T11	T12
Try this:		Use a medium instead of a light for B.					

Buckwheat

3-Unit Grid

Color Illustration: page 12

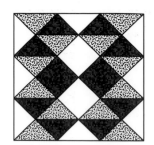
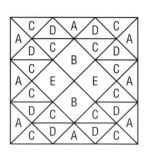

FOR 1 BLOCK:			FINISHED BLOCK SIZE: *Single dimensions in the cutting chart indicate the size of the cut square (3" = 3" x 3")*					
			4½"	6"	7½"	9"	10½"	12"
Light	A: 2 ⊠→⊠		2¾"	3¼"	3¾"	4¼"	4¾"	5¼"
	B: 2 ◇		T5	T7	T9	T11	T12	T14
Medium	C: 3 ⊠→⊠		2¾"	3¼"	3¾"	4¼"	4¾"	5¼"
Dark	D: 2 ⊠→⊠		2¾"	3¼"	3¾"	4¼"	4¾"	5¼"
	E: 2 ◇		T5	T7	T9	T11	T12	T14
Try this:	Use several different mediums for C.							

Card Basket

6-Unit Grid

Color Illustration: page 12

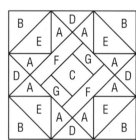

FOR 1 BLOCK:			FINISHED BLOCK SIZE: *Single dimensions in the cutting chart indicate the size of the cut square (3" = 3" x 3")*					
			4½"	6"	7½"	9"	10½"	12"
Light	A: 2 ⊠→⊠		2¾"	3¼"	3¾"	4¼"	4¾"	5¼"
	B: 2 ☐→◻		2⅜"	2⅞"	3⅜"	3⅞"	4⅜"	4⅞"
	C: 1 ◇		T5	T7	T9	T11	T12	T14
Light 2	D: 1 ⊠→⊠		2¾"	3¼"	3¾"	4¼"	4¾"	5¼"
Dark	E: 2 ☐→◻		2⅜"	2⅞"	3⅜"	3⅞"	4⅜"	4⅞"
	F: 2 ◇		T30	T34	T38	T43	T48	T53
	G: 2 ◇		T28	T32	T36	T41	T46	T51
Try this:	Use a medium instead of a light for B and C.							

☐ *Light*   ⣿ *Light 2*   ▦ *Medium*   ▪ *Medium 2*   ■ *Dark*

Carol's Scrap Time Quilt

6-Unit Grid

Color Illustration: page 12

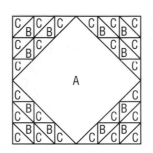

FOR 1 BLOCK:			FINISHED BLOCK SIZE: *Single dimensions in the cutting chart indicate the size of the cut square (3" = 3" x 3")*					
			4½"	6"	7½"	9"	10½"	12"
Light	A: 1		T15	T19	T22	T24	T26	T27
Medium	B: 6		1⅝"	1⅞"	2⅛"	2⅜"	2⅝"	2⅞"
Dark	C: 12		1⅝"	1⅞"	2⅛"	2⅜"	2⅝"	2⅞"
Try this:		Use a medium- or large-scale print for A.						

Castles in Spain

4-Unit Grid

Color Illustration: page 12

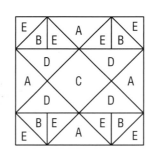

FOR 1 BLOCK:			FINISHED BLOCK SIZE: *Single dimensions in the cutting chart indicate the size of the cut square (3" = 3" x 3")*					
			4"	6"	8"	9"	10"	12"
Light	A: 1		3¼"	4¼"	5¼"	5¾"	6¼"	7¼"
	B: 2		1⅞"	2⅜"	2⅞"	3⅛"	3⅜"	3⅞"
	C: 1		T7	T11	T14	T15	T16	T19
Dark	D: 1		3¼"	4¼"	5¼"	5¾"	6¼"	7¼"
	E: 4		1⅞"	2⅜"	2⅞"	3⅛"	3⅜"	3⅞"
Try this:		Use a medium instead of a dark for E.						

Cats and Mice

6-Unit Grid

Color Illustration: page 12

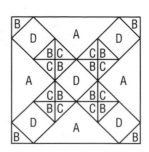
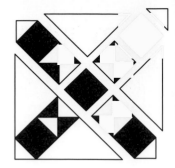

FOR 1 BLOCK:			FINISHED BLOCK SIZE: *Single dimensions in the cutting chart indicate the size of the cut square (3" = 3" x 3")*					
			4½"	6"	7½"	9"	10½"	12"
Light	A: 1		4¼"	5¼"	6¼"	7¼"	8¼"	9¼"
	B: 6		1⅝"	1⅞"	2⅛"	2⅜"	2⅝"	2⅞"
Dark	C: 4		1⅝"	1⅞"	2⅛"	2⅜"	2⅝"	2⅞"
	D: 5		T5	T7	T9	T11	T12	T14
Try this:	Reverse the lights and darks.							

Centennial

4-Unit Grid

Color Illustration: page 12

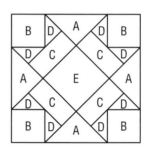

FOR 1 BLOCK:			FINISHED BLOCK SIZE: *Single dimensions in the cutting chart indicate the size of the cut square (3" = 3" x 3")*					
			4"	6"	8"	9"	10"	12"
Light	A: 1		3¼"	4¼"	5¼"	5¾"	6¼"	7¼"
	B: 4		1½"	2"	2½"	2¾"	3"	3½"
	C: 4		T32	T41	T51	T56	T59	T67
Dark	D: 2		2¼"	2¾"	3¼"	3½"	3¾"	4¼"
	E: 1		T7	T11	T14	T15	T16	T19
Try this:	Use a medium instead of a light for C.							

☐ *Light*   ▒ *Light 2*   ▓ *Medium*   ▓ *Medium 2*   ■ *Dark*

Cheyenne

4-Unit Grid

Color Illustration: page 12

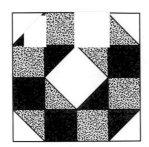
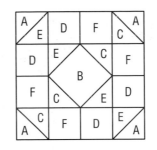
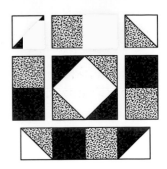

FOR 1 BLOCK:			FINISHED BLOCK SIZE: *Single dimensions in the cutting chart indicate the size of the cut square (3" = 3" x 3")*					
			4"	**6"**	**8"**	**9"**	**10"**	**12"**
Light	A: 2		1⅞"	2⅜"	2⅞"	3⅛"	3⅜"	3⅞"
	B: 1		T7	T11	T14	T15	T16	T19
Medium	C: 2		1⅞"	2⅜"	2⅞"	3⅛"	3⅜"	3⅞"
	D: 4		1½"	2"	2½"	2¾"	3"	3½"
Dark	E: 2		1⅞"	2⅜"	2⅞"	3⅛"	3⅜"	3⅞"
	F: 4		1½"	2"	2½"	2¾"	3"	3½"
Try this:			Use several different mediums and darks.					

Chicago Pavements

8-Unit Grid

Color Illustration: page 12

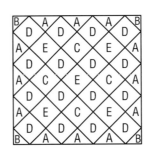
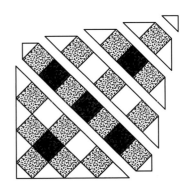

FOR 1 BLOCK:			FINISHED BLOCK SIZE: *Single dimensions in the cutting chart indicate the size of the cut square (3" = 3" x 3")*					
			6"	**8"**	**9"**	**10"**	**12"**	**14"**
Light	A: 3		2¾"	3¼"	3½"	3¾"	4¼"	4¾"
	B: 2		1⅝"	1⅞"	2"	2⅛"	2⅜"	2⅝"
	C: 4		T5	T7	T8	T9	T11	T12
Medium	D: 16		T5	T7	T8	T9	T11	T12
Dark	E: 5		T5	T7	T8	T9	T11	T12
Try this:			Use many different mediums for D.					

Chilkoot Trail

10-Unit Grid
Color Illustration: page 12

FOR 1 BLOCK:			FINISHED BLOCK SIZE: *Single dimensions in the cutting chart indicate the size of the cut square (3" = 3" x 3")*					
			6¼"	7½"	8¾"	10"	12½"	13¾"
Light	A: 6 ⊠→⊠		2½"	2¾"	3"	3¼"	3¾"	4"
	B: 2 ◻→◺		1½"	1⅝"	1¾"	1⅞"	2⅛"	2¼"
Light 2	C: 1 ⊠→⊠		3¾"	4¼"	4¾"	5¼"	6¼"	6¾"
Medium	D: 4 ◇		T38	T43	T48	T53	T61	T65
Dark	E: 1 ⊠→⊠		3¾"	4¼"	4¾"	5¼"	6¼"	6¾"
	F: 2 ⊠→⊠		2½"	2¾"	3"	3¼"	3¾"	4"
	G: 1 ◇		T4	T5	T6	T7	T9	T10
Try this:	Reverse the mediums and darks in every other block.							

Chinook

8-Unit Grid
Color Illustration: page 12

 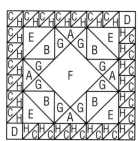 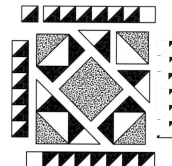

FOR 1 BLOCK:			FINISHED BLOCK SIZE: *Single dimensions in the cutting chart indicate the size of the cut square (3" = 3" x 3")*					
			6"	8"	9"	10"	12"	14"
Light	A: 1 ⊠→⊠		2¾"	3¼"	3½"	3¾"	4¼"	4¾"
	B: 2 ◻→◺		2⅜"	2⅞"	3⅛"	3⅜"	3⅞"	4⅜"
	C: 13 ◻→◺		1⅝"	1⅞"	2"	2⅛"	2⅜"	2⅝"
	D: 2 ◻		1¼"	1½"	1⅝"	1¾"	2"	2¼"
Medium	E: 2 ◻→◺		2⅜"	2⅞"	3⅛"	3⅜"	3⅞"	4⅜"
	F: 1 ◇		T11	T14	T15	T16	T19	T21
Dark	G: 2 ⊠→⊠		2¾"	3¼"	3½"	3¾"	4¼"	4¾"
	H: 13 ◻→◺		1⅝"	1⅞"	2"	2⅛"	2⅜"	2⅝"
Try this:	Use many different darks for H.							

42 ◻ *Light* ▒ *Light 2* ▓ *Medium* ▒ *Medium 2* ■ *Dark*

Christmas Star

6-Unit Grid
Color Illustration: page 12

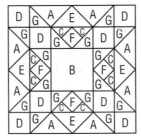

FOR 1 BLOCK:			FINISHED BLOCK SIZE: *Single dimensions in the cutting chart indicate the size of the cut square (3" = 3" x 3")*					
			4½"	**6"**	**7½"**	**9"**	**10½"**	**12"**
Light	A: 2		2¾"	3¼"	3¾"	4¼"	4¾"	5¼"
	B: 1		2"	2½"	3"	3½"	4"	4½"
	C: 2		2"	2¼"	2½"	2¾"	3"	3¼"
	D: 8		1¼"	1½"	1¾"	2"	2¼"	2½"
Medium	E: 1		2¾"	3¼"	3¾"	4¼"	4¾"	5¼"
	F: 4		T1	T2	T4	T5	T6	T7
Dark	G: 8		1⅝"	1⅞"	2⅛"	2⅜"	2⅝"	2⅞"
Try this:		Use a pictorial holiday print for B.						

Chuck a Luck

6-Unit Grid
Color Illustration: page 13

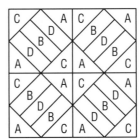

FOR 1 BLOCK:			FINISHED BLOCK SIZE: *Single dimensions in the cutting chart indicate the size of the cut square (3" = 3" x 3")*					
			4½"	**6"**	**7½"**	**9"**	**10½"**	**12"**
Light	A: 4		2"	2⅜"	2¾"	3⅛"	3½"	3⅞"
	B: 6		T29	T33	T37	T42	T47	T52
Dark	C: 4		2"	2⅜"	2¾"	3⅛"	3½"	3⅞"
	D: 6		T29	T33	T37	T42	T47	T52
Try this:		Use a different combination of lights and darks in each quadrant of the block.						

Cobblestones

10-Unit Grid

Color Illustration: page 13

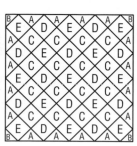 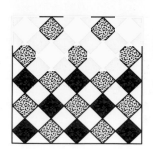 

FOR 1 BLOCK:			**FINISHED BLOCK SIZE:** *Single dimensions in the cutting chart indicate the size of the cut square (3" = 3" x 3")*					
			6¼"	7½"	8¾"	10"	12½"	13¾"
Light	A: 4	⊠→⊠	2½"	2¾"	3"	3¼"	3¾"	4"
	B: 2	◻→◺	1½"	1⅝"	1¾"	1⅞"	2⅛"	2¼"
	C: 16	◇	T4	T5	T6	T7	T9	T10
Medium	D: 12	◇	T4	T5	T6	T7	T9	T10
Dark	E: 13	◇	T4	T5	T6	T7	T9	T10
Try this:			Use many different fabrics for D and E.					

Cock's Comb

4-Unit Grid

Color Illustration: page 13

 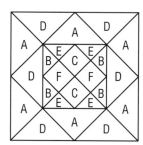 

FOR 2 BLOCKS:			**FINISHED BLOCK SIZE:** *Single dimensions in the cutting chart indicate the size of the cut square (3" = 3" x 3")*					
			4"	6"	8"	9"	10"	12"
Light	A: 3	⊠→⊠	3¼"	4¼"	5¼"	5¾"	6¼"	7¼"
	B: 2	⊠→⊠	2¼"	2¾"	3¼"	3½"	3¾"	4¼"
	C: 4	◇	T2	T5	T7	T8	T9	T11
Dark	D: 3	⊠→⊠	3¼"	4¼"	5¼"	5¾"	6¼"	7¼"
	E: 2	⊠→⊠	2¼"	2¾"	3¼"	3½"	3¾"	4¼"
	F: 4	◇	T2	T5	T7	T8	T9	T11
Try this:			Use a light and a medium instead of a light and a dark in every other block.					

◻ Light   ▦ Light 2   ▓ Medium   ▒ Medium 2   ■ Dark

Coffin Star

4-Unit Grid
Color Illustration: page 13

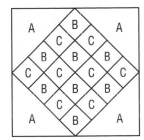

FOR 1 BLOCK:			FINISHED BLOCK SIZE: *Single dimensions in the cutting chart indicate the size of the cut square (3" = 3" x 3")*					
			4"	6"	8"	9"	10"	12"
Light	A: 2		2⅞"	3⅞"	4⅞"	5⅜"	5⅞"	6⅞"
	B: 8		T2	T5	T7	T8	T9	T11
Dark	C: 8		T2	T5	T7	T8	T9	T11
Try this:	Use a different light or a medium for A.							

The Cog Block

4-Unit Grid
Color Illustration: page 13

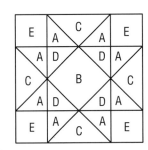

FOR 1 BLOCK:			FINISHED BLOCK SIZE: *Single dimensions in the cutting chart indicate the size of the cut square (3" = 3" x 3")*					
			4"	6"	8"	9"	10"	12"
Light	A: 4		1⅞"	2⅜"	2⅞"	3⅛"	3⅜"	3⅞"
	B: 1		T7	T11	T14	T15	T16	T19
Dark	C: 1		3¼"	4¼"	5¼"	5¾"	6¼"	7¼"
	D: 2		1⅞"	2⅜"	2⅞"	3⅛"	3⅜"	3⅞"
	E: 4		1½"	2"	2½"	2¾"	3"	3½"
Try this:	Reverse the lights and darks in every other block.							

Colonial Garden

4-Unit Grid

Color Illustration: page 13

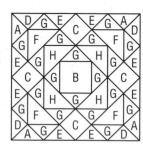

FOR 1 BLOCK:			FINISHED BLOCK SIZE: *Single dimensions in the cutting chart indicate the size of the cut square (3" = 3" x 3")*					
			4"	**6"**	**8"**	**9"**	**10"**	**12"**
Light	A: 1 ⊠→⊠		2¼"	2¾"	3¼"	3½"	3¾"	4¼"
	B: 1 ☐		1½"	2"	2½"	2¾"	3"	3½"
	C: 4 ◇		T2	T5	T7	T8	T9	T11
Light 2	D: 1 ⊠→⊠		2¼"	2¾"	3¼"	3½"	3¾"	4¼"
Medium	E: 2 ⊠→⊠		2¼"	2¾"	3¼"	3½"	3¾"	4¼"
	F: 2 ◻→◸		1⅞"	2⅜"	2⅞"	3⅛"	3⅜"	3⅞"
Medium 2	G: 5 ⊠→⊠		2¼"	2¾"	3¼"	3½"	3¾"	4¼"
Dark	H: 2 ◻→◸		1⅞"	2⅜"	2⅞"	3⅛"	3⅜"	3⅞"
Try this:		Reverse the mediums and darks in every other block.						

Combination Star

6-Unit Grid

Color Illustration: page 13

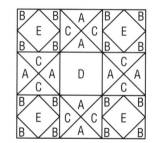

FOR 1 BLOCK:			FINISHED BLOCK SIZE: *Single dimensions in the cutting chart indicate the size of the cut square (3" = 3" x 3")*					
			4½"	**6"**	**7½"**	**9"**	**10½"**	**12"**
Light	A: 2 ⊠→⊠		2¾"	3¼"	3¾"	4¼"	4¾"	5¼"
	B: 8 ◻→◸		1⅝"	1⅞"	2⅛"	2⅜"	2⅝"	2⅞"
Dark	C: 2 ⊠→⊠		2¾"	3¼"	3¾"	4¼"	4¾"	5¼"
	D: 1 ☐		2"	2½"	3"	3½"	4"	4½"
	E: 4 ◇		T5	T7	T9	T11	T12	T14
Try this:		Use a medium instead of a dark for D and E.						

☐ *Light* ▦ *Light 2* ▩ *Medium* ▦ *Medium 2* ■ *Dark*

Connecticut

4-Unit Grid

Color Illustration: page 13

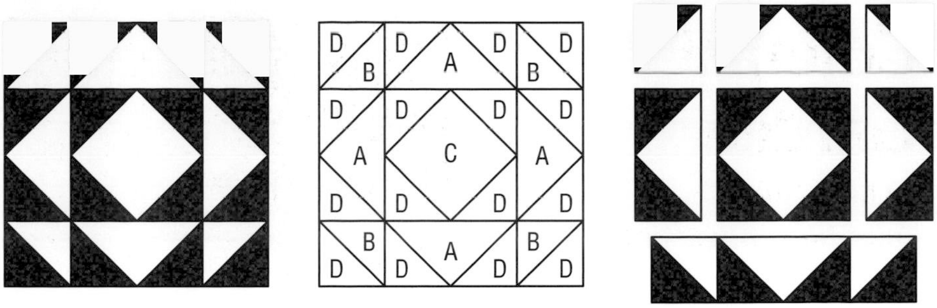

FINISHED BLOCK SIZE:

Single dimensions in the cutting chart indicate the size of the cut square (3" = 3" x 3")

FOR 1 BLOCK:

		4"	6"	8"	9"	10"	12"
Light	A: 1	3¼"	4¼"	5¼"	5¾"	6¼"	7¼"
	B: 2	1⅞"	2⅜"	2⅞"	3⅛"	3⅜"	3⅞"
	C: 1	T7	T11	T14	T15	T16	T19
Dark	D: 8	1⅞"	2⅜"	2⅞"	3⅛"	3⅜"	3⅞"

Try this: Reverse the lights and darks.

Corner Star

8-Unit Grid

Color Illustration: page 13

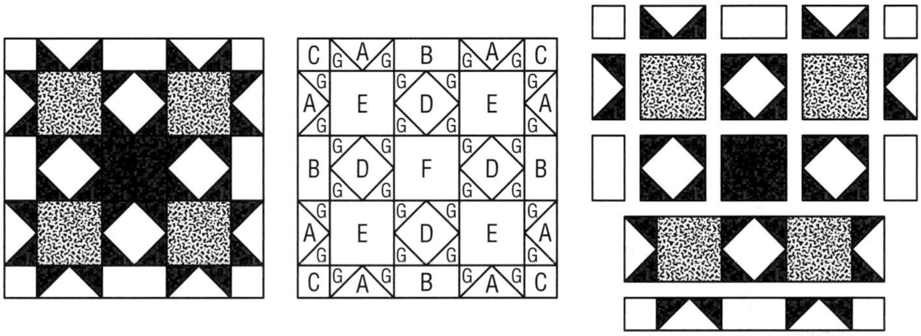

FINISHED BLOCK SIZE:

Single dimensions in the cutting chart indicate the size of the cut square (3" = 3" x 3")

FOR 1 BLOCK:

		6"	8"	9"	10"	12"	14"
Light	A: 2	2¾"	3¼"	3½"	3¾"	4¼"	4¾"
	B: 4	1¼" x 2"	1½" x 2½"	1⅝" x 2¾"	1¾" x 3"	2" x 3½"	2¼" x 4"
	C: 4	1¼"	1½"	1⅝"	1¾"	2"	2¼"
	D: 4	T5	T7	T8	T9	T11	T12
Medium	E: 4	2"	2½"	2¾"	3"	3½"	4"
Dark	F: 1	2"	2½"	2¾"	3"	3½"	4"
	G: 16	1⅝"	1⅞"	2"	2⅛"	2⅜"	2⅝"

Try this: Use several different mediums for E.

Country Checkers

5-Unit Grid

Color Illustration: page 13

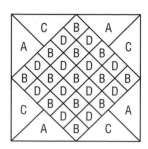

FOR 1 BLOCK:		FINISHED BLOCK SIZE: *Single dimensions in the cutting chart indicate the size of the cut square (3" = 3" x 3")*					
		5"	**6¼"**	**7½"**	**8¾"**	**10"**	**12½"**
Light	A: 1 ⊠→⊠	3¾"	4⅜"	5"	5⅝"	6¼"	7½"
	B: 13 ◇	T2	T4	T5	T6	T7	T9
Light 2	C: 1 ⊠→⊠	3¾"	4⅜"	5"	5⅝"	6¼"	7½"
Dark	D: 12 ◇	T2	T4	T5	T6	T7	T9

Try this: Use many different darks for D.

County Fair

10-Unit Grid

Color Illustration: page 13

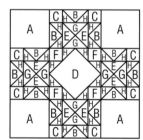
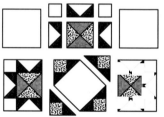

FOR 1 BLOCK:		FINISHED BLOCK SIZE: *Single dimensions in the cutting chart indicate the size of the cut square (3" = 3" x 3")*					
		6¼"	**7½"**	**8¾"**	**10"**	**12½"**	**13¾"**
Light	A: 4 ☐	2⅜"	2¾"	3⅛"	3½"	4¼"	4⅝"
	B: 3 ⊠→⊠	2½"	2¾"	3"	3¼"	3¾"	4"
	C: 8 ☐	1⅛"	1¼"	1⅜"	1½"	1¾"	1⅞"
	D: 1 ◇	T9	T11	T12	T14	T16	T18
Medium	E: 2 ⊠→⊠	2½"	2¾"	3"	3¼"	3¾"	4"
	F: 4 ☐	1⅛"	1¼"	1⅜"	1½"	1¾"	1⅞"
Medium 2	G: 2 ⊠→⊠	2½"	2¾"	3"	3¼"	3¾"	4"
Dark	H: 16 ◺→◹	1½"	1⅝"	1¾"	1⅞"	2⅛"	2¼"

Try this: Use many different mediums for E and G.

☐ *Light* ⬚ *Light 2* ▨ *Medium* ▧ *Medium 2* ■ *Dark*

Courthouse Lawn

8-Unit Grid

Color Illustration: page 13

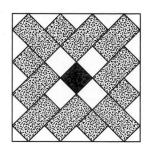
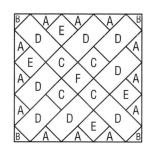
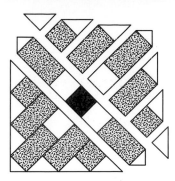

			FINISHED BLOCK SIZE: Single dimensions in the cutting chart indicate the size of the cut square (3" = 3" x 3")					
FOR 1 BLOCK:			**6"**	**8"**	**9"**	**10"**	**12"**	**14"**
Light	A: 3	⊠→⊠	2¾"	3¼"	3½"	3¾"	4¼"	4¾"
	B: 2	◹→◹	1⅝"	1⅞"	2"	2⅛"	2⅜"	2⅝"
	C: 4	◇	T5	T7	T8	T9	T11	T12
Medium	D: 8	◇	T41	T51	T56	T59	T67	T70
	E: 4	◇	T5	T7	T8	T9	T11	T12
Dark	F: 1	◇	T5	T7	T8	T9	T11	T12
Try this:		Use one light for A and B and a different light for C.						

Courthouse Square

6-Unit Grid

Color Illustration: page 14

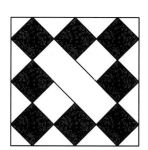
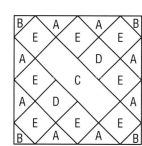

			FINISHED BLOCK SIZE: Single dimensions in the cutting chart indicate the size of the cut square (3" = 3" x 3")					
FOR 1 BLOCK:			**4½"**	**6"**	**7½"**	**9"**	**10½"**	**12"**
Light	A: 2	⊠→⊠	2¾"	3¼"	3¾"	4¼"	4¾"	5¼"
	B: 2	◹→◹	1⅝"	1⅞"	2⅛"	2⅜"	2⅝"	2⅞"
	C: 1	◇	T42	T52	T60	T68	T71	T73
	D: 2	◇	T5	T7	T9	T11	T12	T14
Dark	E: 8	◇	T5	T7	T9	T11	T12	T14
Try this:		Use a medium instead of a dark for E.						

Coxey's Camp

8-Unit Grid

Color Illustration: page 14

 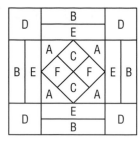 

		FINISHED BLOCK SIZE: Single dimensions in the cutting chart indicate the size of the cut square (3" = 3" x 3")					
FOR 1 BLOCK:		**6"**	**8"**	**9"**	**10"**	**12"**	**14"**
Light	A: 2	2⅜"	2⅞"	3⅛"	3⅜"	3⅞"	4⅜"
	B: 4	1¼" x 3½"	1½" x 4½"	1⅝" x 5"	1¾" x 5½"	2" x 6½"	2¼" x 7½"
	C: 2	T5	T7	T8	T9	T11	T12
Dark	D: 4	2"	2½"	2¾"	3"	3½"	4"
	E: 4	1¼" x 3½"	1½" x 4½"	1⅝" x 5"	1¾" x 5½"	2" x 6½"	2¼" x 7½"
	F: 2	T5	T7	T8	T9	T11	T12
Try this:		Use a medium instead of a light for A.					

Cracker

3-Unit Grid

Color Illustration: page 14

 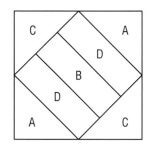 

		FINISHED BLOCK SIZE: Single dimensions in the cutting chart indicate the size of the cut square (3" = 3" x 3")					
FOR 1 BLOCK:		**4½"**	**6"**	**7½"**	**9"**	**10½"**	**12"**
Light	A: 1	3⅛"	3⅞"	4⅝"	5⅜"	6⅛"	6⅞"
	B: 1	T42	T52	T60	T68	T71	T73
Dark	C: 1	3⅛"	3⅞"	4⅝"	5⅜"	6⅛"	6⅞"
	D: 2	T42	T52	T60	T68	T71	T73
Try this:		Use a medium instead of a light for A and B.					

☐ Light   ☐ Light 2   ▦ Medium   ▨ Medium 2   ■ Dark

Cross and Chains

6-Unit Grid

Color Illustration: page 14

 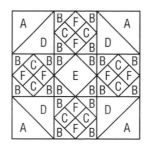 

FOR 1 BLOCK:			FINISHED BLOCK SIZE: *Single dimensions in the cutting chart indicate the size of the cut square (3" = 3" x 3")*					
			4½"	**6"**	**7½"**	**9"**	**10½"**	**12"**
Light	A: 2		2⅜"	2⅞"	3⅜"	3⅞"	4⅜"	4⅞"
	B: 10		1⅝"	1⅞"	2⅛"	2⅜"	2⅝"	2⅞"
	C: 8		T1	T2	T4	T5	T6	T7
Dark	D: 2		2⅜"	2⅞"	3⅜"	3⅞"	4⅜"	4⅞"
	E: 1		T5	T7	T9	T11	T12	T14
	F: 8		T1	T2	T4	T5	T6	T7
Try this:		Use a medium instead of a light for B.						

Cross Roads

6-Unit Grid

Color Illustration: page 14

 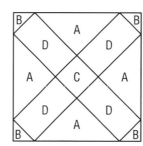 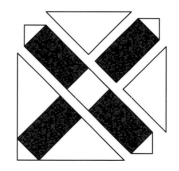

FOR 1 BLOCK:			FINISHED BLOCK SIZE: *Single dimensions in the cutting chart indicate the size of the cut square (3" = 3" x 3")*					
			4½"	**6"**	**7½"**	**9"**	**10½"**	**12"**
Light	A: 1		4¼"	5¼"	6¼"	7¼"	8¼"	9¼"
	B: 2		1⅝"	1⅞"	2⅛"	2⅜"	2⅝"	2⅞"
	C: 1		T5	T7	T9	T11	T12	T14
Dark	D: 4		T41	T51	T59	T67	T70	T72
Try this:		Reverse the lights and darks in every other block.						

Cross Roads to Jericho

3-Unit Grid

Color Illustration: page 14

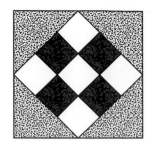
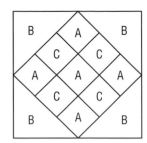
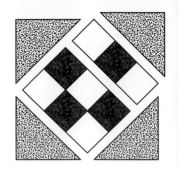

FOR 1 BLOCK:		FINISHED BLOCK SIZE: *Single dimensions in the cutting chart indicate the size of the cut square (3" = 3" x 3")*					
		4½"	6"	7½"	9"	10½"	12"
Light	A: 5	T5	T7	T9	T11	T12	T14
Medium	B: 2	3⅛"	3⅞"	4⅝"	5⅜"	6⅛"	6⅞"
Dark	C: 4	T5	T7	T9	T11	T12	T14
Try this:	Reverse the mediums and darks in every other block.						

Cross Roads to Texas

6-Unit Grid

Color Illustration: page 14

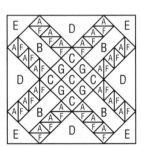

FOR 1 BLOCK:		FINISHED BLOCK SIZE: *Single dimensions in the cutting chart indicate the size of the cut square (3" = 3" x 3")*					
		4½"	6"	7½"	9"	10½"	12"
Light	A: 6	2"	2¼"	2½"	2¾"	3"	3¼"
	B: 4	T29	T33	T37	T42	T47	T52
	C: 5	T1	T2	T4	T5	T6	T7
Medium	D: 1	3½"	4¼"	5"	5¾"	6½"	7¼"
	E: 2	2"	2⅜"	2¾"	3⅛"	3½"	3⅞"
Dark	F: 6	2"	2¼"	2½"	2¾"	3"	3¼"
	G: 4	T1	T2	T4	T5	T6	T7
Try this:	Use one light for A and a different light for B and C.						

☐ Light   ░ Light 2   ▦ Medium   ▨ Medium 2   ■ Dark

Crossed Squares

5-Unit Grid

Color Illustration: page 14

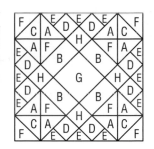

FOR 1 BLOCK:			FINISHED BLOCK SIZE: *Single dimensions in the cutting chart indicate the size of the cut square (3" = 3" x 3")*					
			5"	**6¼"**	**7½"**	**8¾"**	**10"**	**12½"**
Light	A: 4		1⅞"	2⅛"	2⅜"	2⅝"	2⅞"	3⅜"
	B: 4		T32	T36	T41	T46	T51	T59
Light 2	C: 2		1⅞"	2⅛"	2⅜"	2⅝"	2⅞"	3⅜"
	D: 8		T2	T4	T5	T6	T7	T9
Dark	E: 3		2¼"	2½"	2¾"	3"	3¼"	3¾"
	F: 4		1⅞"	2⅛"	2⅜"	2⅝"	2⅞"	3⅜"
	G: 1		T7	T9	T11	T12	T14	T16
	H: 4		T2	T4	T5	T6	T7	T9
Try this:		Use a medium instead of a light for A.						

Crown

6-Unit Grid

Color Illustration: page 14

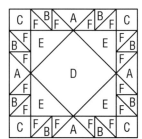

FOR 1 BLOCK:			FINISHED BLOCK SIZE: *Single dimensions in the cutting chart indicate the size of the cut square (3" = 3" x 3")*					
			4½"	**6"**	**7½"**	**9"**	**10½"**	**12"**
Light	A: 1		2¾"	3¼"	3¾"	4¼"	4¾"	5¼"
	B: 4		1⅝"	1⅞"	2⅛"	2⅜"	2⅝"	2⅞"
	C: 4		1¼"	1½"	1¾"	2"	2¼"	2½"
	D: 1		T11	T14	T16	T19	T21	T23
Dark	E: 2		2⅜"	2⅞"	3⅜"	3⅞"	4⅜"	4⅞"
	F: 8		1⅝"	1⅞"	2⅛"	2⅜"	2⅝"	2⅞"
Try this:		Use a different fabric for each "crown."						

53

Crystal Star

4-Unit Grid

Color Illustration: page 14

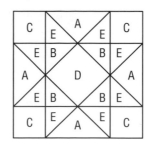

FOR 1 BLOCK:			FINISHED BLOCK SIZE: *Single dimensions in the cutting chart indicate the size of the cut square (3" = 3" x 3")*					
			4"	**6"**	**8"**	**9"**	**10"**	**12"**
Light	A: 1	⊠→⊠	3¼"	4¼"	5¼"	5¾"	6¼"	7¼"
	B: 2	◻→⬒	1⅞"	2⅜"	2⅞"	3⅛"	3⅜"	3⅞"
	C: 4	◻	1½"	2"	2½"	2¾"	3"	3½"
Medium	D: 1	◇	T7	T11	T14	T15	T16	T19
Dark	E: 4	◹→◺	1⅞"	2⅜"	2⅞"	3⅛"	3⅜"	3⅞"
Try this:			Use one light for A and C and a different light for B.					

Darien's Dilemma

5-Unit Grid

Color Illustration: page 14

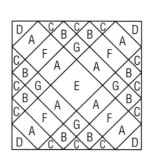

FOR 1 BLOCK:			FINISHED BLOCK SIZE: *Single dimensions in the cutting chart indicate the size of the cut square (3" = 3" x 3")*					
			5"	**6¼"**	**7½"**	**8¾"**	**10"**	**12½"**
Light	A: 8	◇	T32	T36	T41	T46	T51	T59
	B: 8	◇	T2	T4	T5	T6	T7	T9
Dark	C: 3	⊠→⊠	2¼"	2½"	2¾"	3"	3¼"	3¾"
	D: 2	◻→⬒	1⅞"	2⅛"	2⅜"	2⅝"	2⅞"	3⅜"
	E: 1	◇	T7	T9	T11	T12	T14	T16
	F: 4	◇	T32	T36	T41	T46	T51	T59
	G: 4	◇	T2	T4	T5	T6	T7	T9
Try this:			Use a light and a medium instead of a light and a dark for every other block.					

◻ *Light* ⬚ *Light 2* ▦ *Medium* ▨ *Medium 2* ■ *Dark*

Denali

8-Unit Grid
Color Illustration: page 14

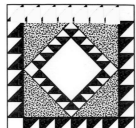 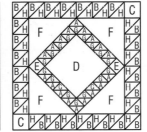

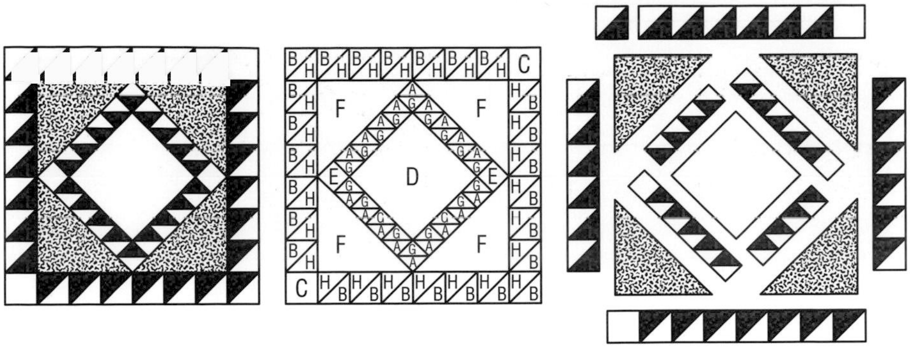

FOR 2 BLOCKS:			FINISHED BLOCK SIZE: *Single dimensions in the cutting chart indicate the size of the cut square (3" = 3" x 3")*					
			6"	**8"**	**9"**	**10"**	**12"**	**14"**
Light	A: 9	⊠→⊠	2"	2¼"	2⅜"	2½"	2¾"	3"
	B: 26	◺→◺	1⅝"	1⅞"	2"	2⅛"	2⅜"	2⅝"
	C: 4	▢	1¼"	1½"	1⅝"	1¾"	2"	2¼"
	D: 2	◇	T11	T14	T15	T16	T19	T21
	E: 4	◇	T1	T2	T3	T4	T5	T6
Medium	F: 4	◻→◺	3⅛"	3⅞"	4¼"	4⅝"	5⅜"	6⅛"
Dark	G: 9	⊠→⊠	2"	2¼"	2⅜"	2½"	2¾"	3"
	H: 26	◺→◺	1⅝"	1⅞"	2"	2⅛"	2⅜"	2⅝"
Try this:			Use many different darks for G and H.					

A Design for Patriotism

8-Unit Grid
Color Illustration: page 15

 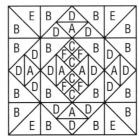 

FOR 2 BLOCKS:			FINISHED BLOCK SIZE: *Single dimensions in the cutting chart indicate the size of the cut square (3" = 3" x 3")*					
			6"	**8"**	**9"**	**10"**	**12"**	**14"**
Light	A: 3	⊠→⊠	2¾"	3¼"	3½"	3¾"	4¼"	4¾"
	B: 16	◻→◺	2⅜"	2⅞"	3⅛"	3⅜"	3⅞"	4⅜"
	C: 8	◇	T1	T2	T3	T4	T5	T6
Dark	D: 7	⊠→⊠	2¾"	3¼"	3½"	3¾"	4¼"	4¾"
	E: 4	◻→◺	2⅜"	2⅞"	3⅛"	3⅜"	3⅞"	4⅜"
	F: 8	◇	T1	T2	T3	T4	T5	T6
Try this:			Use a medium for A and several different lights for B.					

Devil's Claws II

8-Unit Grid

Color Illustration: page 15

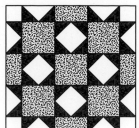
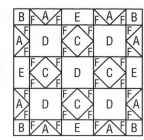

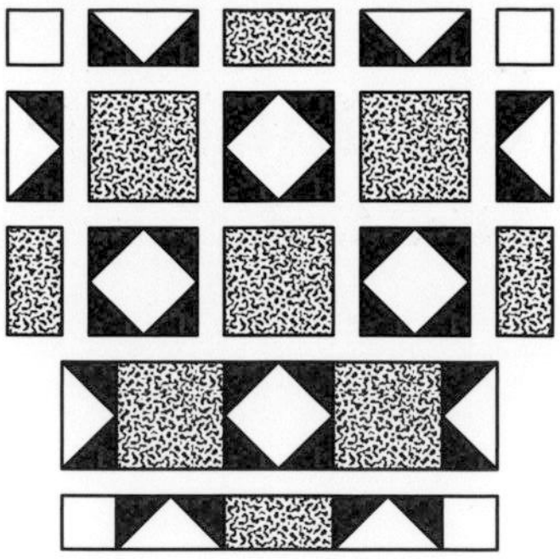

FOR 1 BLOCK:			FINISHED BLOCK SIZE: *Single dimensions in the cutting chart indicate the size of the cut square (3" = 3" x 3")*					
			6"	**8"**	**9"**	**10"**	**12"**	**14"**
Light	A: 2	⊠→⊠	2¾"	3¼"	3½"	3¾"	4¼"	4¾"
	B: 4	□	1¼"	1½"	1⅝"	1¾"	2"	2¼"
	C: 4	◇	T5	T7	T8	T9	T11	T12
Medium	D: 5	□	2"	2½"	2¾"	3"	3½"	4"
	E: 4	▭	1¼" x 2"	1½" x 2½"	1⅝" x 2¾"	1¾" x 3"	2" x 3½"	2¼" x 4"
Dark	F: 16	◻→◺	1⅝"	1⅞"	2"	2⅛"	2⅜"	2⅝"

Try this: Use several different mediums for D.

Domino and Square

5-Unit Grid

Color Illustration: page 15

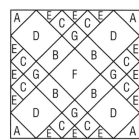

FOR 1 BLOCK:			FINISHED BLOCK SIZE: *Single dimensions in the cutting chart indicate the size of the cut square (3" = 3" x 3")*					
			5"	**6¼"**	**7½"**	**8¾"**	**10"**	**12½"**
Light	A: 2	◻→◺	1⅞"	2⅛"	2⅜"	2⅝"	2⅞"	3⅜"
	B: 4	◇	T32	T36	T41	T46	T51	T59
	C: 8	◇	T2	T4	T5	T6	T7	T9
Medium	D: 4	◇	T7	T9	T11	T12	T14	T16
Dark	E: 3	⊠→⊠	2¼"	2½"	2¾"	3"	3¼"	3¾"
	F: 1	◇	T7	T9	T11	T12	T14	T16
	G: 4	◇	T2	T4	T5	T6	T7	T9

Try this: Reverse the darks and mediums.

□ Light	⬜ Light 2	▦ Medium	▩ Medium 2	■ Dark

Double Cross

4-Unit Grid

Color Illustration: page 15

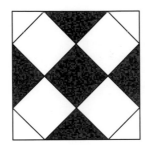
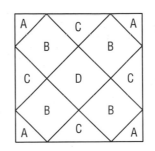

FINISHED BLOCK SIZE:						
Single dimensions in the cutting chart indicate the size of the cut square (3" = 3" x 3")						
FOR 1 BLOCK:		4"	6"	8"	9"	10"	12"
Light	A: 2	1⅞"	2⅜"	2⅞"	3⅛"	3⅜"	3⅞"
	B: 4	T7	T11	T14	T15	T16	T19
Dark	C: 1	3¼"	4¼"	5¼"	5¾"	6¼"	7¼"
	D: 1	T7	T11	T14	T15	T16	T19
Try this:	Use a medium instead of a light for A.						

The Double Square

10-Unit Grid

Color Illustration: page 15

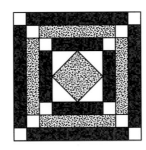
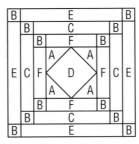
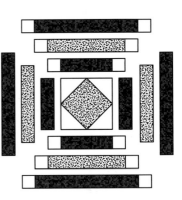

FINISHED BLOCK SIZE:						
Single dimensions in the cutting chart indicate the size of the cut square (3" = 3" x 3")						
FOR 1 BLOCK:		6¼"	7½"	8¾"	10"	12½"	13¾"
Light	A: 2	2⅛"	2⅜"	2⅝"	2⅞"	3⅜"	3⅝"
	B: 12	1⅛"	1¼"	1⅜"	1½"	1¾"	1⅞"
Medium	C: 4	1⅛" x 4¼"	1¼" x 5"	1⅜" x 5¾"	1½" x 6½"	1¾" x 8"	1⅞" x 8¾"
	D: 1	T9	T11	T12	T14	T16	T18
Dark	E: 4	1⅛" x 5½"	1¼" x 6½"	1⅜" x 7½"	1½" x 8½"	1¾" x 10½"	1⅞" x 11½"
	F: 4	1⅛" x 3"	1¼" x 3½"	1⅜" x 4"	1½" x 4½"	1¾" x 5½"	1⅞" x 6"
Try this:	Reverse the mediums and darks in every other block.						

Double T

4-Unit Grid

Color Illustration: page 15

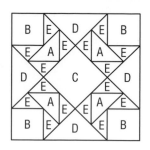

			FINISHED BLOCK SIZE: *Single dimensions in the cutting chart indicate the size of the cut square (3" = 3" x 3")*					
FOR 1 BLOCK:			**4"**	**6"**	**8"**	**9"**	**10"**	**12"**
Light	A: 2		1⅞"	2⅜"	2⅞"	3⅛"	3⅜"	3⅞"
	B: 4		1½"	2"	2½"	2¾"	3"	3½"
	C: 1		T7	T11	T14	T15	T16	T19
Dark	D: 1		3¼"	4¼"	5¼"	5¾"	6¼"	7¼"
	E: 4		2¼"	2¾"	3¼"	3½"	3¾"	4¼"
Try this:			Make two of the "T's" from one dark and the other two from a medium or a different dark.					

Eagle's Nest

8-Unit Grid

Color Illustration: page 15

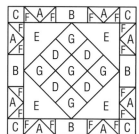

			FINISHED BLOCK SIZE: *Single dimensions in the cutting chart indicate the size of the cut square (3" = 3" x 3")*					
FOR 1 BLOCK:			**6"**	**8"**	**9"**	**10"**	**12"**	**14"**
Light	A: 2		2¾"	3¼"	3½"	3¾"	4¼"	4¾"
	B: 4		1¼" x 2"	1½" x 2½"	1⅝" x 2¾"	1¾" x 3"	2" x 3½"	2¼" x 4"
	C: 4		1¼"	1½"	1⅝"	1¾"	2"	2¼"
	D: 4		T5	T7	T8	T9	T11	T12
Medium	E: 2		3⅛"	3⅞"	4¼"	4⅝"	5⅜"	6⅛"
Dark	F: 8		1⅝"	1⅞"	2"	2⅛"	2⅜"	2⅝"
	G: 5		T5	T7	T8	T9	T11	T12
Try this:			Use one light for A, B, and C and a different light for D.					

58   ☐ *Light*   ▦ *Light 2*   ▨ *Medium*   ▨ *Medium 2*   ■ *Dark*

Economy

4-Unit Grid

Color Illustration: page 15

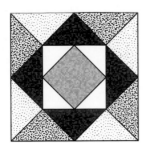 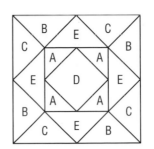 

		FINISHED BLOCK SIZE: *Single dimensions in the cutting chart indicate the size of the cut square (3" = 3" x 3")*					
FOR 1 BLOCK:		**4"**	**6"**	**8"**	**9"**	**10"**	**12"**
Light	A: 2	1⅞"	2⅜"	2⅞"	3⅛"	3⅜"	3⅞"
Light 2	B: 1	3¼"	4¼"	5¼"	5¾"	6¼"	7¼"
Medium	C: 1	3¼"	4¼"	5¼"	5¾"	6¼"	7¼"
Medium 2	D: 1	T7	T11	T14	T15	T16	T19
Dark	E: 1	3¼"	4¼"	5¼"	5¾"	6¼"	7¼"
Try this:	Use several different fabrics for B and C.						

Eight Pointed Star

4-Unit Grid

Color Illustration: page 15

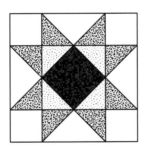 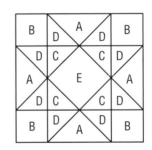 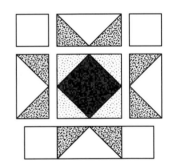

		FINISHED BLOCK SIZE: *Single dimensions in the cutting chart indicate the size of the cut square (3" = 3" x 3")*					
FOR 1 BLOCK:		**4"**	**6"**	**8"**	**9"**	**10"**	**12"**
Light	A: 1	3¼"	4¼"	5¼"	5¾"	6¼"	7¼"
	B: 4	1½"	2"	2½"	2¾"	3"	3½"
Light 2	C: 2	1⅞"	2⅜"	2⅞"	3⅛"	3⅜"	3⅞"
Medium	D: 4	1⅞"	2⅜"	2⅞"	3⅛"	3⅜"	3⅞"
Dark	E: 1	T7	T11	T14	T15	T16	T19
Try this:	Reverse the lights and the dark.						

Eva's Delight

6-Unit Grid
Color Illustration: page 15

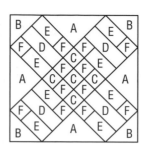

FOR 1 BLOCK:			**FINISHED BLOCK SIZE:** *Single dimensions in the cutting chart indicate the size of the cut square (3" = 3" x 3")*					
			4½"	**6"**	**7½"**	**9"**	**10½"**	**12"**
Light	A: 1	⊠→⊠	3½"	4¼"	5"	5¾"	6½"	7¼"
	B: 2	◻→◸	2"	2⅜"	2¾"	3⅛"	3½"	3⅞"
	C: 5	◇	T1	T2	T4	T5	T6	T7
Medium	D: 4	◇	T29	T33	T37	T42	T47	T52
	E: 8	◇	T28	T32	T36	T41	T46	T51
Dark	F: 12	◇	T1	T2	T4	T5	T6	T7
Try this:			Use one medium for D and a different medium for E.					

Federal Square

4-Unit Grid
Color Illustration: page 15

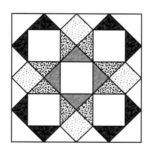
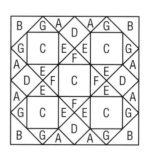

FOR 1 BLOCK:			**FINISHED BLOCK SIZE:** *Single dimensions in the cutting chart indicate the size of the cut square (3" = 3" x 3")*					
			4"	**6"**	**8"**	**9"**	**10"**	**12"**
Light	A: 2	⊠→⊠	2¼"	2¾"	3¼"	3½"	3¾"	4¼"
	B: 2	◻→◸	1⅞"	2⅜"	2⅞"	3⅛"	3⅜"	3⅞"
	C: 5	◻	1½"	2"	2½"	2¾"	3"	3½"
Light 2	D: 4	◇	T2	T5	T7	T8	T9	T11
Medium	E: 2	⊠→⊠	2¼"	2¾"	3¼"	3½"	3¾"	4¼"
Medium 2	F: 1	⊠→⊠	2¼"	2¾"	3¼"	3½"	3¾"	4¼"
Dark	G: 2	⊠→⊠	2¼"	2¾"	3¼"	3½"	3¾"	4¼"
Try this:			Use a dark instead of a light for the center square.					

◻ Light   ▨ Light 2   ▨ Medium   ▨ Medium 2   ■ Dark

Five Crosses

8-Unit Grid

Color Illustration: page 15

FOR 1 BLOCK:			FINISHED BLOCK SIZE: Single dimensions in the cutting chart indicate the size of the cut square (3" = 3" x 3")					
			6"	8"	9"	10"	12"	14"
Light	A: 3		2¾"	3¼"	3½"	3¾"	4¼"	4¾"
	B: 2		1⅝"	1⅞"	2"	2⅛"	2⅜"	2⅝"
	C: 4		T5	T7	T8	T9	T11	T12
Dark	D: 5		T42	T52	T57	T60	T68	T71
	E: 6		T5	T7	T8	T9	T11	T12

Try this: Reverse the lights and darks in every other block.

Five Diamonds

6-Unit Grid

Color Illustration: page 16

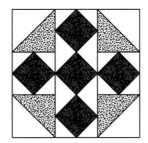

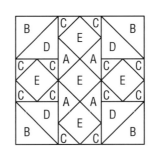

FOR 1 BLOCK:			FINISHED BLOCK SIZE: Single dimensions in the cutting chart indicate the size of the cut square (3" = 3" x 3")					
			4½"	6"	7½"	9"	10½"	12"
Light	A: 1		2¾"	3¼"	3¾"	4¼"	4¾"	5¼"
	B: 2		2⅜"	2⅞"	3⅜"	3⅞"	4⅜"	4⅞"
	C: 6		1⅝"	1⅞"	2⅛"	2⅜"	2⅝"	2⅞"
Medium	D: 2		2⅜"	2⅞"	3⅜"	3⅞"	4⅜"	4⅞"
Dark	E: 5		T5	T7	T9	T11	T12	T14

Try this: Use one light for A and C and a different light for B.

Five Spot

6-Unit Grid

Color Illustration: page 16

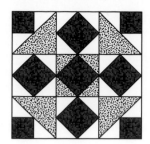
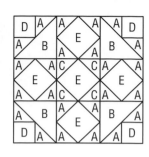
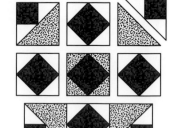

FOR 1 BLOCK:		FINISHED BLOCK SIZE: *Single dimensions in the cutting chart indicate the size of the cut square (3" = 3" x 3")*					
		4½"	6"	7½"	9"	10½"	12"
Light	A: 12 ◻→◨	1⅝"	1⅞"	2⅛"	2⅜"	2⅝"	2⅞"
Medium	B: 2 ◻→◨	2⅜"	2⅞"	3⅜"	3⅞"	4⅜"	4⅞"
	C: 2 ◻→◨	1⅝"	1⅞"	2⅛"	2⅜"	2⅝"	2⅞"
Dark	D: 4 ◻	1¼"	1½"	1¾"	2"	2¼"	2½"
	E: 5 ◇	T5	T7	T9	T11	T12	T14
Try this:	Use one dark for D and a different dark for E.						

Flying Shuttles

6-Unit Grid

Color Illustration: page 16

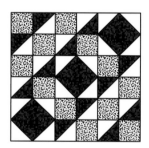
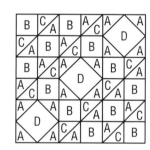
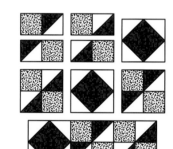

FOR 1 BLOCK:		FINISHED BLOCK SIZE: *Single dimensions in the cutting chart indicate the size of the cut square (3" = 3" x 3")*					
		4½"	6"	7½"	9"	10½"	12"
Light	A: 12 ◻→◨	1⅝"	1⅞"	2⅛"	2⅜"	2⅝"	2⅞"
Medium	B: 12 ◻	1¼"	1½"	1¾"	2"	2¼"	2½"
Dark	C: 6 ◻→◨	1⅝"	1⅞"	2⅛"	2⅜"	2⅝"	2⅞"
	D: 3 ◇	T5	T7	T9	T11	T12	T14
Try this:	Use many different lights and mediums.						

◻ Light · ▦ Light 2 · ▨ Medium · ▨ Medium 2 · ■ Dark

Four Squares

6-Unit Grid

Color Illustration: page 16

 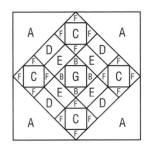 

FOR 1 BLOCK:		FINISHED BLOCK SIZE: *Single dimensions in the cutting chart indicate the size of the cut square (3" = 3" x 3")*					
		4½"	6"	7½"	9"	10½"	12"
Light	A: 2	3⅛"	3⅞"	4⅝"	5⅜"	6⅛"	6⅞"
	B: 1	2"	2¼"	2½"	2¾"	3"	3¼"
	C: 4	1¼"	1½"	1¾"	2"	2¼"	2½"
	D: 4	T28	T32	T36	T41	T46	T51
Medium	E: 4	T28	T32	T36	T41	T46	T51
Dark	F: 4	2"	2¼"	2½"	2¾"	3"	3¼"
	G: 1	1¼"	1½"	1¾"	2"	2¼"	2½"
Try this:		Use a medium instead of a light for A.					

Four-Four Time

4-Unit Grid

Color Illustration: page 16

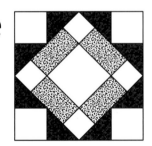 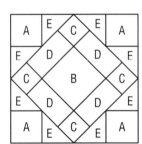 

FOR 1 BLOCK:		FINISHED BLOCK SIZE: *Single dimensions in the cutting chart indicate the size of the cut square (3" = 3" x 3")*					
		4"	6"	8"	9"	10"	12"
Light	A: 4	1½"	2"	2½"	2¾"	3"	3½"
	B: 1	T7	T11	T14	T15	T16	T19
	C: 4	T2	T5	T7	T8	T9	T11
Medium	D: 4	T32	T41	T51	T56	T59	T67
Dark	E: 4	1⅞"	2⅜"	2⅞"	3⅛"	3⅜"	3⅞"
Try this:		Use one light for A and B and a different light for C.					

Fox Paws

8-Unit Grid

Color Illustration: page 16

FOR 1 BLOCK:			FINISHED BLOCK SIZE: *Single dimensions in the cutting chart indicate the size of the cut square (3" = 3" x 3")*					
			6"	**8"**	**9"**	**10"**	**12"**	**14"**
Light	A: 1	⊠→⊠	4¼"	5¼"	5¾"	6¼"	7¼"	8¼"
	B: 12	◹→◹	1⅝"	1⅞"	2"	2⅛"	2⅜"	2⅝"
Medium	C: 8	◹→◹	1⅝"	1⅞"	2"	2⅛"	2⅜"	2⅝"
	D: 4	☐	1¼"	1½"	1⅝"	1¾"	2"	2¼"
	E: 1	◇	T11	T14	T15	T16	T19	T21
Dark	F: 4	◹→◹	2⅜"	2⅞"	3⅛"	3⅜"	3⅞"	4⅜"

Try this: Use a medium instead of a light for A.

NOTE: *This block is listed as "Unnamed" in Barbara Brackman's* Encyclopedia of Pieced Quilt Patterns; *the source given is Robert Bishop and Elizabeth Safanda's book* A Gallery of Amish Quilts: Design Diversity from a Plain People, *published in 1976. For this book, I've chosen to call the block "Fox Paws."*

Friendship Chain

8-Unit Grid

Color Illustration: page 16

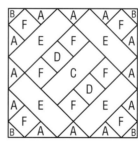

FOR 1 BLOCK:			FINISHED BLOCK SIZE: *Single dimensions in the cutting chart indicate the size of the cut square (3" = 3" x 3")*					
			6"	**8"**	**9"**	**10"**	**12"**	**14"**
Light	A: 3	⊠→⊠	2¾"	3¼"	3½"	3¾"	4¼"	4¾"
	B: 2	⊠→◹	1⅝"	1⅞"	2"	2⅛"	2⅜"	2⅝"
	C: 1	◇	T42	T52	T57	T60	T68	T71
	D: 2	◇	T5	T7	T8	T9	T11	T12
Dark	E: 4	◇	T42	T52	T57	T60	T68	T71
	F: 8	◇	T5	T7	T8	T9	T11	T12

Try this: Use a light and a medium instead of a light and a dark for every other block.

☐ *Light* ⬚ *Light 2* ▨ *Medium* ▥ *Medium 2* ■ *Dark*

The Friendship Quilt

6-Unit Grid

Color Illustration: page 16

 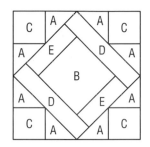 

FOR 1 BLOCK:			**FINISHED BLOCK SIZE:** *Single dimensions in the cutting chart indicate the size of the cut square (3" = 3" x 3")*					
			4½"	**6"**	**7½"**	**9"**	**10½"**	**12"**
Light	A: 4		2"	2⅜"	2¾"	3⅛"	3½"	3⅞"
	B: 1		T11	T14	T16	T19	T21	T23
Dark	C: 4		1⅝"	2"	2⅜"	2¾"	3⅛"	3½"
	D: 2		T31	T35	T40	T45	T50	T55
	E: 2		T30	T34	T38	T43	T48	T53
Try this:		Use one dark for C and a different dark for D and E.						

Friendship Quilt II

10-Unit Grid

Color Illustration: page 16

 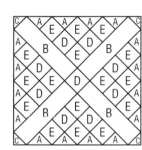 

FOR 1 BLOCK:			**FINISHED BLOCK SIZE:** *Single dimensions in the cutting chart indicate the size of the cut square (3" = 3" x 3")*					
			6¼"	**7½"**	**8¾"**	**10"**	**12½"**	**13¾"**
Light	A: 4		2½"	2¾"	3"	3¼"	3¾"	4"
	B: 4		T38	T43	T48	T53	T61	T65
Medium	C: 2		1½"	1⅝"	1¾"	1⅞"	2⅛"	2¼"
	D: 9		T4	T5	T6	T7	T9	T10
Dark	E: 16		T4	T5	T6	T7	T9	T10
Try this:		Use many different fabrics for D and E.						

65

Garden of Eden

5-Unit Grid

Color Illustration: page 16

  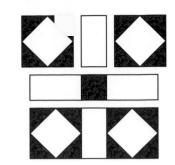

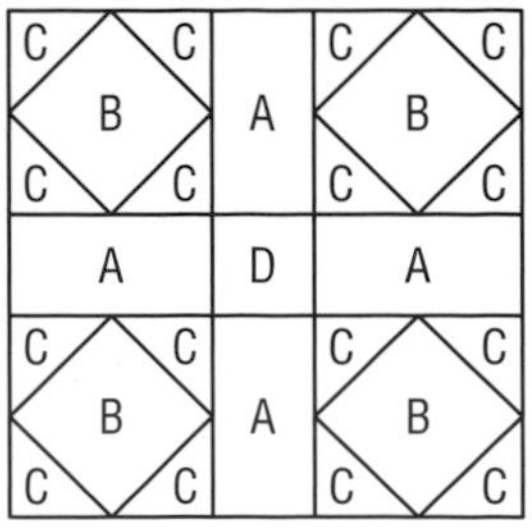

FOR 1 BLOCK:			FINISHED BLOCK SIZE: *Single dimensions in the cutting chart indicate the size of the cut square (3" = 3" x 3")*					
			5"	6¼"	7½"	8¾"	10"	12½"
Light	A: 4	▭	1½" x 2½"	1¾" x 3"	2" x 3½"	2¼" x 4"	2½" x 4½"	3" x 5½"
	B: 4	◇	T7	T9	T11	T12	T14	T16
Dark	C: 8	◹→◸	1⅞"	2⅛"	2⅜"	2⅝"	2⅞"	3⅜"
	D: 1	▢	1½"	1¾"	2"	2¼"	2½"	3"
Try this:		Reverse the lights and darks in every other block.						

The Garden Patch

8-Unit Grid

Color Illustration: page 16

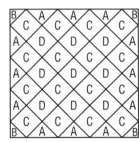 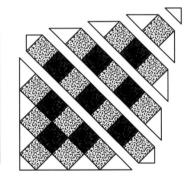

FOR 1 BLOCK:			FINISHED BLOCK SIZE: *Single dimensions in the cutting chart indicate the size of the cut square (3" = 3" x 3")*					
			6"	8"	9"	10"	12"	14"
Light	A: 3	⊠→⊠	2¾"	3¼"	3½"	3¾"	4¼"	4¾"
	B: 2	◹→◸	1⅝"	1⅞"	2"	2⅛"	2⅜"	2⅝"
Medium	C: 16	◇	T5	T7	T8	T9	T11	T12
Dark	D: 9	◇	T5	T7	T8	T9	T11	T12
Try this:		Use many different mediums for C.						

▢ Light · ▦ Light 2 · ▨ Medium · ▩ Medium 2 · ■ Dark

Gem Block

6-Unit Grid

Color Illustration: page 16

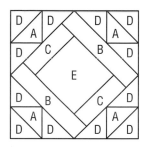

FOR 1 BLOCK:			FINISHED BLOCK SIZE: *Single dimensions in the cutting chart indicate the size of the cut square (3" = 3" x 3")*					
			4½"	6"	7½"	9"	10½"	12"
Light	A: 2		2"	2⅜"	2¾"	3⅛"	3½"	3⅞"
	B: 2		T31	T35	T40	T45	T50	T55
	C: 2		T30	T34	T38	T43	T48	T53
Dark	D: 6		2"	2⅜"	2¾"	3⅛"	3½"	3⅞"
	E: 1		T11	T14	T16	T19	T21	T23
Try this:		Use a large-scale print for E.						

Georgetown Circle

4-Unit Grid

Color Illustration: page 17

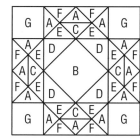

FOR 1 BLOCK:			FINISHED BLOCK SIZE: *Single dimensions in the cutting chart indicate the size of the cut square (3" = 3" x 3")*					
			4"	6"	8"	9"	10"	12"
Light	A: 3		2¼"	2¾"	3¼"	3½"	3¾"	4¼"
	B: 1		T7	T11	T14	T15	T16	T19
Medium	C: 1		2¼"	2¾"	3¼"	3½"	3¾"	4¼"
	D: 2		1⅞"	2⅜"	2⅞"	3⅛"	3⅜"	3⅞"
Medium 2	E: 2		2¼"	2¾"	3¼"	3½"	3¾"	4¼"
Dark	F: 2		2¼"	2¾"	3¼"	3½"	3¾"	4¼"
	G: 4		1½"	2"	2½"	2¾"	3"	3½"
Try this:		Use one light for A and a different light for B.						

Glacier Bay

6-Unit Grid

Color Illustration: page 17

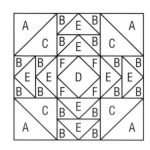

FOR 1 BLOCK:			FINISHED BLOCK SIZE: *Single dimensions in the cutting chart indicate the size of the cut square (3" = 3" x 3")*					
			4½"	6"	7½"	9"	10½"	12"
Light	A: 2	◻→◿	2⅜"	2⅞"	3⅜"	3⅞"	4⅜"	4⅞"
	B: 8	◻→◿	1⅝"	1⅞"	2⅛"	2⅜"	2⅝"	2⅞"
Medium	C: 2	◻→◿	2⅜"	2⅞"	3⅜"	3⅞"	4⅜"	4⅞"
	D: 1	◇	T5	T7	T9	T11	T12	T14
Dark	E: 2	⊠→⊠	2¾"	3¼"	3¾"	4¼"	4¾"	5¼"
	F: 2	◻→◿	1⅝"	1⅞"	2⅛"	2⅜"	2⅝"	2⅞"
Try this:		Reverse the mediums and darks.						

Gold Rush

8-Unit Grid

Color Illustration: page 17

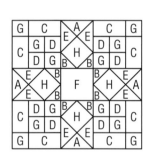
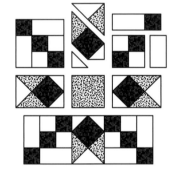

FOR 1 BLOCK:			FINISHED BLOCK SIZE: *Single dimensions in the cutting chart indicate the size of the cut square (3" = 3" x 3")*					
			6"	8"	9"	10"	12"	14"
Light	A: 1	⊠→⊠	2¾"	3¼"	3½"	3¾"	4¼"	4¾"
	B: 4	◻→◿	1⅝"	1⅞"	2"	2⅛"	2⅜"	2⅝"
	C: 8	▭	1¼" x 2"	1½" x 2½"	1⅝" x 2¾"	1¾" x 3"	2" x 3½"	2¼" x 4"
	D: 8	◻	1¼"	1½"	1⅝"	1¾"	2"	2¼"
Medium	E: 2	⊠→⊠	2¾"	3¼"	3½"	3¾"	4¼"	4¾"
	F: 1	◻	2"	2½"	2¾"	3"	3½"	4"
Dark	G: 12	◻	1¼"	1½"	1⅝"	1¾"	2"	2¼"
	H: 4	◇	T5	T7	T8	T9	T11	T12
Try this:		Use one light for A, C, and D and a different light for B.						

◻ Light ▢ Light 2 ▨ Medium ▧ Medium 2 ■ Dark

Good Fortune

6-Unit Grid

Color Illustration: page 17

 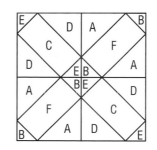 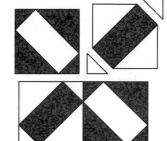

			FINISHED BLOCK SIZE:					
			Single dimensions in the cutting chart indicate the size of the cut square (3" = 3" x 3")					
FOR 1 BLOCK:			4½"	6"	7½"	9"	10½"	12"
Light	A: 2		2⅜"	2⅞"	3⅜"	3⅞"	4⅜"	4⅞"
	B: 2		1⅝"	1⅞"	2⅛"	2⅜"	2⅝"	2⅞"
	C: 2		T41	T51	T59	T67	T70	T72
Dark	D: 2		2⅜"	2⅞"	3⅜"	3⅞"	4⅜"	4⅞"
	E: 2		1⅝"	1⅞"	2⅛"	2⅜"	2⅝"	2⅞"
	F: 2		T41	T51	T59	T67	T70	T72
Try this:			Use a different combination of light and dark fabrics in each quadrant of the block.					

Goose in the Pond

5-Unit Grid

Color Illustration: page 17

 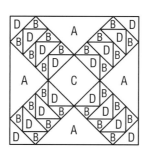 

			FINISHED BLOCK SIZE:					
			Single dimensions in the cutting chart indicate the size of the cut square (3" = 3" x 3")					
FOR 1 BLOCK:			5"	6¼"	7½"	8¾"	10"	12½"
Light	A: 1		4¼"	5"	5¾"	6½"	7¼"	8¾"
	B: 6		2¼"	2½"	2¾"	3"	3¼"	3¾"
	C: 1		T7	T9	T11	T12	T14	T16
Dark	D: 8		1⅞"	2⅛"	2⅜"	2⅝"	2⅞"	3⅜"
Try this:			Use one light for A and a different light for B and C.					

Grandmother's Cross

4-Unit Grid

Color Illustration: page 17

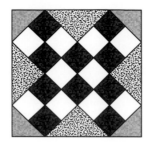 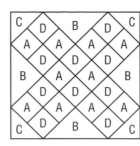 

FOR 1 BLOCK:			FINISHED BLOCK SIZE: *Single dimensions in the cutting chart indicate the size of the cut square (3" = 3" x 3")*					
			4"	**6"**	**8"**	**9"**	**10"**	**12"**
Light	A: 10	◇	T2	T5	T7	T8	T9	T11
Medium	B: 1	⊠→⊠	3¼"	4¼"	5¼"	5¾"	6¼"	7¼"
Medium 2	C: 2	◻→◺	1⅞"	2⅜"	2⅞"	3⅛"	3⅜"	3⅞"
Dark	D: 10	◇	T2	T5	T7	T8	T9	T11
Try this:		Use several different darks for D.						

Grandmother's Pride

6-Unit Grid

Color Illustration: page 17

 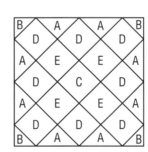 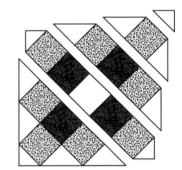

FOR 1 BLOCK:			FINISHED BLOCK SIZE: *Single dimensions in the cutting chart indicate the size of the cut square (3" = 3" x 3")*					
			4½"	**6"**	**7½"**	**9"**	**10½"**	**12"**
Light	A: 2	⊠→⊠	2¾"	3¼"	3¾"	4¼"	4¾"	5¼"
	B: 2	◻→◺	1⅝"	1⅞"	2⅛"	2⅜"	2⅝"	2⅞"
	C: 1	◇	T5	T7	T9	T11	T12	T14
Medium	D: 8	◇	T5	T7	T9	T11	T12	T14
Dark	E: 4	◇	T5	T7	T9	T11	T12	T14
Try this:		Reverse the lights and mediums in every other block.						

☐ *Light* ░ *Light 2* ▥ *Medium* ▦ *Medium 2* ■ *Dark*

Grecian Square II

4-Unit Grid

Color Illustration: page 17

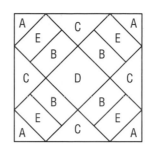

		FINISHED BLOCK SIZE:					
FOR 1 BLOCK:		*Single dimensions in the cutting chart indicate the size of the cut square (3" = 3" x 3")*					
		4"	6"	8"	9"	10"	12"
Light	A: 2	1⅞"	2⅜"	2⅞"	3⅛"	3⅜"	3⅞"
	B: 4	T32	T41	T51	T56	T59	T67
Dark	C: 1	3¼"	4¼"	5¼"	5¾"	6¼"	7¼"
	D: 1	T7	T11	T14	T15	T16	T19
	E: 4	T32	T41	T51	T56	T59	T67

Try this: Use a medium instead of a dark for C and D.

The H Square Quilt

6-Unit Grid

Color Illustration: page 17

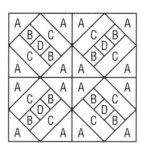

		FINISHED BLOCK SIZE:					
FOR 1 BLOCK:		*Single dimensions in the cutting chart indicate the size of the cut square (3" = 3" x 3")*					
		4½"	6"	7½"	9"	10½"	12"
Light	A: 8	2"	2⅜"	2¾"	3⅛"	3½"	3⅞"
	B: 8	T1	T2	T4	T5	T6	T7
Dark	C: 8	T29	T33	T37	T42	T47	T52
	D: 4	T1	T2	T4	T5	T6	T7

Try this: Use a different combination of light and dark fabrics for each "H."

71

Hazy Daisy

4-Unit Grid

Color Illustration: page 17

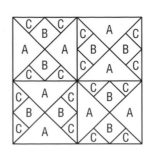

FOR 1 BLOCK:		FINISHED BLOCK SIZE: *Single dimensions in the cutting chart indicate the size of the cut square (3" = 3" x 3")*					
		4"	6"	8"	9"	10"	12"
Light	A: 2 ⊠→⊠	3¼"	4¼"	5¼"	5¾"	6¼"	7¼"
Medium	B: 8 ◇	T2	T5	T7	T8	T9	T11
Dark	C: 4 ⊠→⊠	2¼"	2¾"	3¼"	3½"	3¾"	4¼"
Try this:	Use different light, medium, and dark fabrics in each quadrant of the block.						

Hill and Crag

5-Unit Grid

Color Illustration: page 17

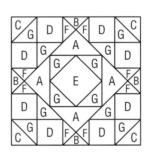

FOR 1 BLOCK:		FINISHED BLOCK SIZE: *Single dimensions in the cutting chart indicate the size of the cut square (3" = 3" x 3")*					
		5"	6¼"	7½"	8¾"	10"	12½"
Light	A: 1 ⊠→⊠	3¼"	3¾"	4¼"	4¾"	5¼"	6¼"
	B: 1 ⊠→⊠	2¼"	2½"	2¾"	3"	3¼"	3¾"
	C: 2 ◻→◹	1⅞"	2⅛"	2⅜"	2⅝"	2⅞"	3⅜"
	D: 8 ◻	1½"	1¾"	2"	2¼"	2½"	3"
	E: 1 ◇	T7	T9	T11	T12	T14	T16
Dark	F: 2 ⊠→⊠	2¼"	2½"	2¾"	3"	3¼"	3¾"
	G: 6 ◻→◹	1⅞"	2⅛"	2⅜"	2⅝"	2⅞"	3⅜"
Try this:	Use a medium instead of a light for A and C.						

☐ *Light* ⊡ *Light 2* ▨ *Medium* ▦ *Medium 2* ■ *Dark*

Hither and Yon

4-Unit Grid

Color Illustration: page 17

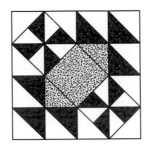 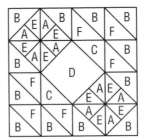 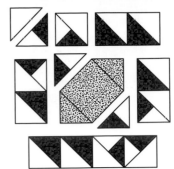

FOR 1 BLOCK:			FINISHED BLOCK SIZE: *Single dimensions in the cutting chart indicate the size of the cut square (3" = 3" x 3")*					
			4"	**6"**	**8"**	**9"**	**10"**	**12"**
Light	A: 2		2¼"	2¾"	3¼"	3½"	3¾"	4¼"
	B: 6		1⅞"	2⅜"	2⅞"	3⅛"	3⅜"	3⅞"
Medium	C: 1		1⅞"	2⅜"	2⅞"	3⅛"	3⅜"	3⅞"
	D: 1		T7	T11	T14	T15	T16	T19
Dark	E: 2		2¼"	2¾"	3¼"	3½"	3¾"	4¼"
	F: 3		1⅞"	2⅜"	2⅞"	3⅛"	3⅜"	3⅞"

Try this: Use one dark for E and a different dark for F.

Home Circle

5-Unit Grid

Color Illustration: page 18

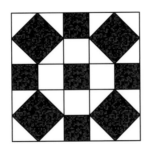 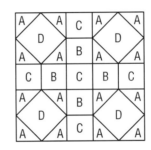 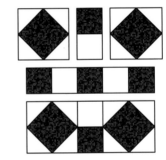

FOR 1 BLOCK:			FINISHED BLOCK SIZE: *Single dimensions in the cutting chart indicate the size of the cut square (3" = 3" x 3")*					
			5"	**6¼"**	**7½"**	**8¾"**	**10"**	**12½"**
Light	A: 8		1⅞"	2⅛"	2⅜"	2⅝"	2⅞"	3⅜"
	B: 4		1½"	1¾"	2"	2¼"	2½"	3"
Dark	C: 5		1½"	1¾"	2"	2¼"	2½"	3"
	D: 4		T7	T9	T11	T12	T14	T16

Try this: Reverse the lights and darks.

Hour Glass II

4-Unit Grid

Color Illustration: page 18

 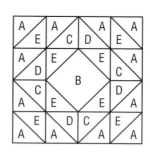 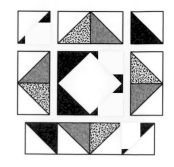

FOR 1 BLOCK:			FINISHED BLOCK SIZE: *Single dimensions in the cutting chart indicate the size of the cut square (3" = 3" x 3")*					
			4"	**6"**	**8"**	**9"**	**10"**	**12"**
Light	A: 6		1⅞"	2⅜"	2⅞"	3⅛"	3⅜"	3⅞"
	B: 1		T7	T11	T14	T15	T16	T19
Medium	C: 2		1⅞"	2⅜"	2⅞"	3⅛"	3⅜"	3⅞"
Medium 2	D: 2		1⅞"	2⅜"	2⅞"	3⅛"	3⅜"	3⅞"
Dark	E: 4		1⅞"	2⅜"	2⅞"	3⅛"	3⅜"	3⅞"
Try this:			Use several different mediums for C and D.					

The House Jack Built

6-Unit Grid

Color Illustration: page 18

 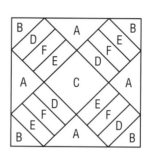 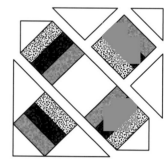

FOR 1 BLOCK:			FINISHED BLOCK SIZE: *Single dimensions in the cutting chart indicate the size of the cut square (3" = 3" x 3")*					
			4½"	**6"**	**7½"**	**9"**	**10½"**	**12"**
Light	A: 1		3½"	4¼"	5"	5¾"	6½"	7¼"
	B: 2		2"	2⅜"	2¾"	3⅛"	3½"	3⅞"
	C: 1		T8	T11	T13	T15	T17	T19
Medium	D: 4		T29	T33	T37	T42	T47	T52
Medium 2	E: 4		T29	T33	T37	T42	T47	T52
Dark	F: 4		T29	T33	T37	T42	T47	T52
Try this:			Use one light for A and B and a different light for C.					

☐ *Light*　▨ *Light 2*　▦ *Medium*　▨ *Medium 2*　■ *Dark*

Iditarod Trail

10-Unit Grid

Color Illustration: page 18

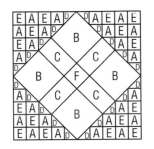

FOR 1 BLOCK:			FINISHED BLOCK SIZE: *Single dimensions in the cutting chart indicate the size of the cut square (3" = 3" x 3")*					
			6¼"	7½"	8¾"	10"	12½"	13¾"
Light	A: 24	□	1⅛"	1¼"	1⅜"	1½"	1¾"	1⅞"
	B: 4	◇	T9	T11	T12	T14	T16	T18
Medium	C: 4	◇	T36	T41	T46	T51	T59	T63
Dark	D: 10	□→◩	1½"	1⅝"	1¾"	1⅞"	2⅛"	2¼"
	E: 16	□	1⅛"	1¼"	1⅜"	1½"	1¾"	1⅞"
	F: 1	◇	T4	T5	T6	T7	T9	T10
Try this:	Use many different darks for E.							

Illinois

6-Unit Grid

Color Illustration: page 18

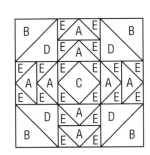
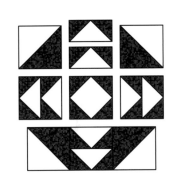

FOR 1 BLOCK:			FINISHED BLOCK SIZE: *Single dimensions in the cutting chart indicate the size of the cut square (3" = 3" x 3")*					
			4½"	6"	7½"	9"	10½"	12"
Light	A: 2	⊠→⊠	2¾"	3¼"	3¾"	4¼"	4¾"	5¼"
	B: 2	�«→◧	2⅜"	2⅞"	3⅜"	3⅞"	4⅜"	4⅞"
	C: 1	◇	T5	T7	T9	T11	T12	T14
Dark	D: 2	◺→◹	2⅜"	2⅞"	3⅜"	3⅞"	4⅜"	4⅞"
	E: 10	◺→◹	1⅝"	1⅞"	2⅛"	2⅜"	2⅝"	2⅞"
Try this:	Use lights and mediums instead of lights and darks.							

Imperial T

6-Unit Grid

Color Illustration: page 18

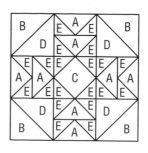

FOR 1 BLOCK:			**FINISHED BLOCK SIZE:** *Single dimensions in the cutting chart indicate the size of the cut square (3" = 3" x 3")*					
			4½"	**6"**	**7½"**	**9"**	**10½"**	**12"**
Light	A: 2		2¾"	3¼"	3¾"	4¼"	4¾"	5¼"
	B: 2		2⅜"	2⅞"	3⅜"	3⅞"	4⅜"	4⅞"
	C: 1		T5	T7	T9	T11	T12	T14
Dark	D: 2		2⅜"	2⅞"	3⅜"	3⅞"	4⅜"	4⅞"
	E: 10		1⅝"	1⅞"	2⅛"	2⅜"	2⅝"	2⅞"
Try this:		Reverse the lights and darks in every other block.						

Improved Four Patch

4-Unit Grid

Color Illustration: page 18

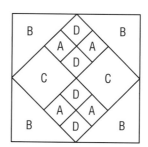

FOR 1 BLOCK:			**FINISHED BLOCK SIZE:** *Single dimensions in the cutting chart indicate the size of the cut square (3" = 3" x 3")*					
			4"	**6"**	**8"**	**9"**	**10"**	**12"**
Light	A: 4		T2	T5	T7	T8	T9	T11
Light 2	B: 2		2⅞"	3⅞"	4⅞"	5⅜"	5⅞"	6⅞"
Medium	C: 2		T7	T11	T14	T15	T16	T19
Dark	D: 4		T2	T5	T7	T8	T9	T11
Try this:		Reverse the dark and medium in every other block.						

☐ Light · ⊡ Light 2 · ▦ Medium · ▨ Medium 2 · ■ Dark

Indian Maze

8-Unit Grid

Color Illustration: page 18

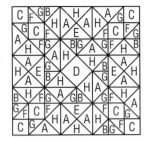

FOR 1 BLOCK:			**FINISHED BLOCK SIZE:** *Single dimensions in the cutting chart indicate the size of the cut square (3" = 3" x 3")*					
			6"	**8"**	**9"**	**10"**	**12"**	**14"**
Light	A: 4	⊠→⊠	2¾"	3¼"	3½"	3¾"	4¼"	4¾"
	B: 4	◻→◻	1⅝"	1⅞"	2"	2⅛"	2⅜"	2⅝"
	C: 8	◻	1¼"	1½"	1⅝"	1¾"	2"	2¼"
	D: 1	◇	T5	T7	T8	T9	T11	T12
Light 2	E: 1	⊠→⊠	2¾"	3¼"	3½"	3¾"	4¼"	4¾"
	F: 6	◻→◻	1⅝"	1⅞"	2"	2⅛"	2⅜"	2⅝"
Medium	G: 8	◻→◻	1⅝"	1⅞"	2"	2⅛"	2⅜"	2⅝"
Dark	H: 4	⊠→⊠	2¾"	3¼"	3½"	3¾"	4¼"	4¾"
Try this:		Use several different darks for H.						

Indiana Puzzle

6-Unit Grid

Color Illustration: page 18

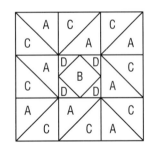

FOR 1 BLOCK:			**FINISHED BLOCK SIZE:** *Single dimensions in the cutting chart indicate the size of the cut square (3" = 3" x 3")*					
			4½"	**6"**	**7½"**	**9"**	**10½"**	**12"**
Light	A: 4	◻→◻	2⅜"	2⅞"	3⅜"	3⅞"	4⅜"	4⅞"
	B: 1	◇	T5	T7	T9	T11	T12	T14
Dark	C: 4	◻→◻	2⅜"	2⅞"	3⅜"	3⅞"	4⅜"	4⅞"
	D: 2	◻→◻	1⅝"	1⅞"	2⅛"	2⅜"	2⅝"	2⅞"
Try this:		Reverse the lights and darks in every other block.						

Indiana Puzzle II

4-Unit Grid

Color Illustration: page 18

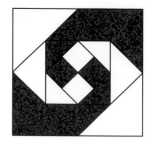
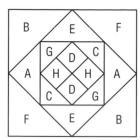

FOR 2 BLOCKS:			FINISHED BLOCK SIZE: *Single dimensions in the cutting chart indicate the size of the cut square (3" = 3" x 3")*					
			4"	**6"**	**8"**	**9"**	**10"**	**12"**
Light	A: 1	⊠→⊠	3¼"	4¼"	5¼"	5¾"	6¼"	7¼"
	B: 2	◻→◺	2⅞"	3⅞"	4⅞"	5⅜"	5⅞"	6⅞"
	C: 2	◻→◺	1⅞"	2⅜"	2⅞"	3⅛"	3⅜"	3⅞"
	D: 4	◇	T2	T5	T7	T8	T9	T11
Dark	E: 1	⊠→⊠	3¼"	4¼"	5¼"	5¾"	6¼"	7¼"
	F: 2	◻→◺	2⅞"	3⅞"	4⅞"	5⅜"	5⅞"	6⅞"
	G: 2	◻→◺	1⅞"	2⅜"	2⅞"	3⅛"	3⅜"	3⅞"
	H: 4	◇	T2	T5	T7	T8	T9	T11
Try this:			Use a different dark for each "curl."					

Inside Passage

5-Unit Grid

Color Illustration: page 18

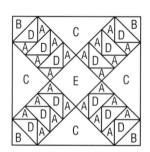

FOR 1 BLOCK:			FINISHED BLOCK SIZE: *Single dimensions in the cutting chart indicate the size of the cut square (3" = 3" x 3")*					
			5"	**6¼"**	**7½"**	**8¾"**	**10"**	**12½"**
Light	A: 6	⊠→⊠	2¼"	2½"	2¾"	3"	3¼"	3¾"
	B: 2	◻→◺	1⅞"	2⅛"	2⅜"	2⅝"	2⅞"	3⅜"
Medium	C: 1	⊠→⊠	4¼"	5"	5¾"	6½"	7¼"	8¾"
Dark	D: 6	◻→◺	1⅞"	2⅛"	2⅜"	2⅝"	2⅞"	3⅜"
	E: 1	◇	T7	T9	T11	T12	T14	T16
Try this:			Use several different lights for A.					

Legend: ☐ Light · ⣿ Light 2 · ▦ Medium · ▓ Medium 2 · ■ Dark

Irish Chain

8-Unit Grid
Color Illustration: page 18

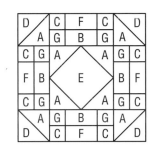
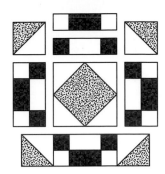

			FINISHED BLOCK SIZE:					
			Single dimensions in the cutting chart indicate the size of the cut square (3" = 3" x 3")					
FOR 1 BLOCK:			**6"**	**8"**	**9"**	**10"**	**12"**	**14"**
Light	A: 4		2⅜"	2⅞"	3⅛"	3⅜"	3⅞"	4⅜"
	B: 4		1¼" x 2"	1½" x 2½"	1⅝" x 2¾"	1¾" x 3"	2" x 3½"	2¼" x 4"
	C: 8		1¼"	1½"	1⅝"	1¾"	2"	2¼"
Medium	D: 2		2⅜"	2⅞"	3⅛"	3⅜"	3⅞"	4⅜"
	E: 1		T11	T14	T15	T16	T19	T21
Dark	F: 4		1¼" x 2"	1½" x 2½"	1⅝" x 2¾"	1¾" x 3"	2" x 3½"	2¼" x 4"
	G: 8		1¼"	1½"	1⅝"	1¾"	2"	2¼"
Try this:			Use one medium for D and a different medium for E.					

Jack in the Pulpit

4-Unit Grid
Color Illustration: page 19

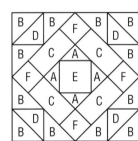

			FINISHED BLOCK SIZE:					
			Single dimensions in the cutting chart indicate the size of the cut square (3" = 3" x 3")					
FOR 1 BLOCK:			**4"**	**6"**	**8"**	**9"**	**10"**	**12"**
Light	A: 1		2¼"	2¾"	3¼"	3½"	3¾"	4¼"
	B: 6		1⅞"	2⅜"	2⅞"	3⅛"	3⅜"	3⅞"
	C: 4		T32	T41	T51	T56	T59	T67
Dark	D: 2		1⅞"	2⅜"	2⅞"	3⅛"	3⅜"	3⅞"
	E: 1		1½"	2"	2½"	2¾"	3"	3½"
	F: 4		T2	T5	T7	T8	T9	T11
Try this:			Use a medium instead of a light for C.					

Jack's Delight

3-Unit Grid

Color Illustration: page 19

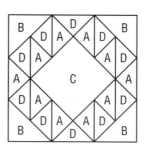

| | | **FINISHED BLOCK SIZE:** | | | | | |
| | | *Single dimensions in the cutting chart indicate the size of the cut square (3" = 3" x 3")* | | | | | |
FOR 2 BLOCKS:		**4½"**	**6"**	**7½"**	**9"**	**10½"**	**12"**
Light	A: 5 ⊠→⊠	2¾"	3¼"	3¾"	4¼"	4¾"	5¼"
	B: 4 ◻→◻	2⅜"	2⅞"	3⅜"	3⅞"	4⅜"	4⅞"
Medium	C: 2 ◇	T11	T14	T16	T19	T21	T23
Dark	D: 5 ⊠→⊠	2¾"	3¼"	3¾"	4¼"	4¾"	5¼"
Try this:	Reverse the lights and darks in every other block.						

Jefferson City

3-Unit Grid

Color Illustration: page 19

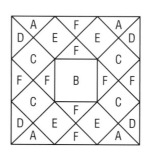

| | | **FINISHED BLOCK SIZE:** | | | | | |
| | | *Single dimensions in the cutting chart indicate the size of the cut square (3" = 3" x 3")* | | | | | |
FOR 1 BLOCK:		**4½"**	**6"**	**7½"**	**9"**	**10½"**	**12"**
Light	A: 1 ⊠→⊠	2¾"	3¼"	3¾"	4¼"	4¾"	5¼"
	B: 1 ◻	2"	2½"	3"	3½"	4"	4½"
	C: 4 ◇	T5	T7	T9	T11	T12	T14
Medium	D: 1 ⊠→⊠	2¾"	3¼"	3¾"	4¼"	4¾"	5¼"
	E: 4 ◇	T5	T7	T9	T11	T12	T14
Dark	F: 2 ⊠→⊠	2¾"	3¼"	3¾"	4¼"	4¾"	5¼"
Try this:	Use several different mediums for D and E.						

◻ Light   ▦ Light 2   ▨ Medium   ▩ Medium 2   ■ Dark

Joseph's Coat

5-Unit Grid

Color Illustration: page 19

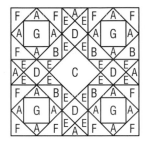

FOR 1 BLOCK:			FINISHED BLOCK SIZE: *Single dimensions in the cutting chart indicate the size of the cut square (3" = 3" x 3")*					
			5"	**6¼"**	**7½"**	**8¾"**	**10"**	**12½"**
Light	A: 5		2¼"	2½"	2¾"	3"	3¼"	3¾"
	B: 2		1⅞"	2⅛"	2⅜"	2⅝"	2⅞"	3⅜"
	C: 1		T7	T9	T11	T12	T14	T16
	D: 4		T2	T4	T5	T6	T7	T9
Dark	E: 4		2¼"	2½"	2¾"	3"	3¼"	3¾"
	F: 6		1⅞"	2⅛"	2⅜"	2⅝"	2⅞"	3⅜"
	G: 4		1½"	1¾"	2"	2¼"	2½"	3"
Try this:		Use one light for A and a different light or a medium for B, C and D.						

July Fourth

4-Unit Grid

Color Illustration: page 19

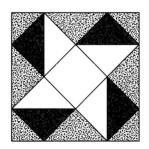
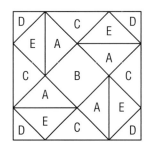

FOR 1 BLOCK:			FINISHED BLOCK SIZE: *Single dimensions in the cutting chart indicate the size of the cut square (3" = 3" x 3")*					
			4"	**6"**	**8"**	**9"**	**10"**	**12"**
Light	A: 1		3¼"	4¼"	5¼"	5¾"	6¼"	7¼"
	B: 1		T7	T11	T14	T15	T16	T19
Medium	C: 1		3¼"	4¼"	5¼"	5¾"	6¼"	7¼"
	D: 2		1⅞"	2⅜"	2⅞"	3⅛"	3⅜"	3⅞"
Dark	E: 1		3¼"	4¼"	5¼"	5¾"	6¼"	7¼"
Try this:		Use a different combination of mediums and darks in every block.						

81

Juneau

8-Unit Grid

Color Illustration: page 19

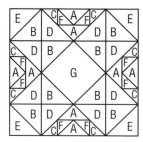

			FINISHED BLOCK SIZE: *Single dimensions in the cutting chart indicate the size of the cut square (3" = 3" x 3")*				
FOR 1 BLOCK:		**6"**	**8"**	**9"**	**10"**	**12"**	**14"**
Light	A: 2 ⊠→⊠	2¾"	3¼"	3½"	3¾"	4¼"	4¾"
	B: 4 ◱→◩	2⅜"	2⅞"	3⅛"	3⅜"	3⅞"	4⅜"
	C: 4 ◱→�￩	1⅝"	1⅞"	2"	2⅛"	2⅜"	2⅝"
Medium	D: 4 ◱→◩	2⅜"	2⅞"	3⅛"	3⅜"	3⅞"	4⅜"
Dark	E: 2 ◱→◩	2⅜"	2⅞"	3⅛"	3⅜"	3⅞"	4⅜"
	F: 4 ◱→◩	1⅝"	1⅞"	2"	2⅛"	2⅜"	2⅝"
	G: 1 ◇	T11	T14	T15	T16	T19	T21
Try this:	Reverse the mediums and darks.						

Kansas Star

6-Unit Grid

Color Illustration: page 19

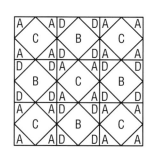

			FINISHED BLOCK SIZE: *Single dimensions in the cutting chart indicate the size of the cut square (3" = 3" x 3")*				
FOR 1 BLOCK:		**4½"**	**6"**	**7½"**	**9"**	**10½"**	**12"**
Light	A: 10 ◱→◩	1⅝"	1⅞"	2⅛"	2⅜"	2⅝"	2⅞"
	B: 4 ◇	T5	T7	T9	T11	T12	T14
Medium	C: 5 ◇	T5	T7	T9	T11	T12	T14
Dark	D: 8 ◱→◩	1⅝"	1⅞"	2⅛"	2⅜"	2⅝"	2⅞"
Try this:	Reverse the lights and mediums in every other block.						

☐ *Light* ▦ *Light 2* ▨ *Medium* ▨ *Medium 2* ■ *Dark*

Kentucky Crossroads

6-Unit Grid

Color Illustration: page 19

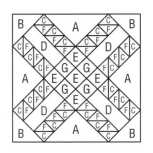

		FINISHED BLOCK SIZE:					
		Single dimensions in the cutting chart indicate the size of the cut square (3" = 3" x 3")					
FOR 1 BLOCK:		**4½"**	**6"**	**7½"**	**9"**	**10½"**	**12"**
Light	A: 1	3½"	4¼"	5"	5¾"	6½"	7¼"
	B: 2	2"	2⅜"	2¾"	3⅛"	3½"	3⅞"
	C: 6	2"	2¼"	2½"	2¾"	3"	3¼"
	D: 4	T29	T33	T37	T42	T47	T52
	E: 5	T1	T2	T4	T5	T6	T7
Dark	F: 6	2"	2¼"	2½"	2¾"	3"	3¼"
	G: 4	T1	T2	T4	T5	T6	T7
Try this:	Use several different darks for F.						

Ladies' Aid Block

6-Unit Grid

Color Illustration: page 19

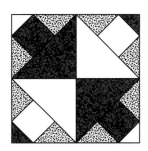
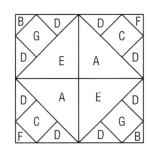
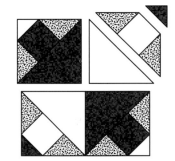

		FINISHED BLOCK SIZE:					
		Single dimensions in the cutting chart indicate the size of the cut square (3" = 3" x 3")					
FOR 1 BLOCK:		**4½"**	**6"**	**7½"**	**9"**	**10½"**	**12"**
Light	A: 1	3⅛"	3⅞"	4⅝"	5⅜"	6⅛"	6⅞"
	B: 1	1⅝"	1⅞"	2⅛"	2⅜"	2⅝"	2⅞"
	C: 2	T5	T7	T9	T11	T12	T14
Medium	D: 2	2¾"	3¼"	3¾"	4¼"	4¾"	5¼"
Dark	E: 1	3⅛"	3⅞"	4⅝"	5⅜"	6⅛"	6⅞"
	F: 1	1⅝"	1⅞"	2⅛"	2⅜"	2⅝"	2⅞"
	G: 2	T5	T7	T9	T11	T12	T14
Try this:	Use a different combination of lights, mediums and darks in each quadrant of the block.						

Lincoln

5-Unit Grid

Color Illustration: page 19

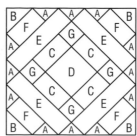

			FINISHED BLOCK SIZE: *Single dimensions in the cutting chart indicate the size of the cut square (3" = 3" x 3")*					
FOR 1 BLOCK:			**5"**	**6¼"**	**7½"**	**8¾"**	**10"**	**12½"**
Light	A: 3 ⊠→⊠		2¼"	2½"	2¾"	3"	3¼"	3¾"
	B: 2 □→□		1⅞"	2⅛"	2⅜"	2⅝"	2⅞"	3⅜"
	C: 4 ◇		T32	T36	T41	T46	T51	T59
Dark	D: 1 ◇		T7	T9	T11	T12	T14	T16
	E: 4 ◇		T34	T38	T43	T48	T53	T61
	F: 4 ◇		T32	T36	T41	T46	T51	T59
	G: 4 ◇		T2	T4	T5	T6	T7	T9
Try this:			Use a light and a medium instead of a light and a dark in every other block.					

Lola

4-Unit Grid

Color Illustration: page 19

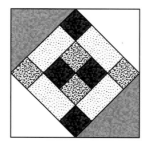
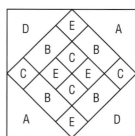
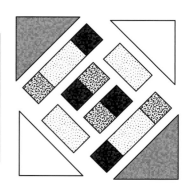

			FINISHED BLOCK SIZE: *Single dimensions in the cutting chart indicate the size of the cut square (3" = 3" x 3")*					
FOR 1 BLOCK:			**4"**	**6"**	**8"**	**9"**	**10"**	**12"**
Light	A: 1 □→□		2⅞"	3⅞"	4⅞"	5⅜"	5⅞"	6⅞"
Light 2	B: 4 ◇		T32	T41	T51	T56	T59	T67
Medium	C: 4 ◇		T2	T5	T7	T8	T9	T11
Medium 2	D: 1 □→□		2⅞"	3⅞"	4⅞"	5⅜"	5⅞"	6⅞"
Dark	E: 4 ◇		T2	T5	T7	T8	T9	T11
Try this:			Use different fabrics for A and D in every block.					

84

□ *Light*　▦ *Light 2*　▨ *Medium*　▧ *Medium 2*　■ *Dark*

Magic Cross

4-Unit Grid

Color Illustration: page 19

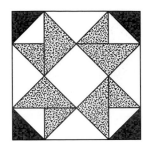
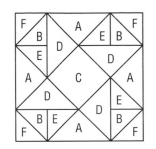

			FINISHED BLOCK SIZE:				
			Single dimensions in the cutting chart indicate the size of the cut square (3" = 3" x 3")				
FOR 1 BLOCK:			**4"**	**6"**	**8"**	**9"**	**10"**	**12"**
Light	A: 1 ⊠→⊠		3¼"	4¼"	5¼"	5¾"	6¼"	7¼"
	B: 2 ◻→◺		1⅞"	2⅜"	2⅞"	3⅛"	3⅜"	3⅞"
	C: 1 ◇		T7	T11	T14	T15	T16	T19
Medium	D: 1 ⊠→⊠		3¼"	4¼"	5¼"	5¾"	6¼"	7¼"
	E: 2 ◻→◺		1⅞"	2⅜"	2⅞"	3⅛"	3⅜"	3⅞"
Dark	F: 2 ◻→◺		1⅞"	2⅜"	2⅞"	3⅛"	3⅜"	3⅞"
Try this:	Reverse the mediums and darks.							

Malvina's Chain

3-Unit Grid

Color Illustration: page 20

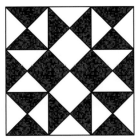
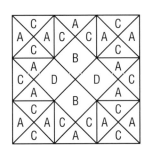

			FINISHED BLOCK SIZE:				
			Single dimensions in the cutting chart indicate the size of the cut square (3" = 3" x 3")				
FOR 2 BLOCKS:			**4½"**	**6"**	**7½"**	**9"**	**10½"**	**12"**
Light	A: 7 ⊠→⊠		2¾"	3¼"	3¾"	4¼"	4¾"	5¼"
	B: 4 ◇		T5	T7	T9	T11	T12	T14
Dark	C: 7 ⊠→⊠		2¾"	3¼"	3¾"	4¼"	4¾"	5¼"
	D: 4 ◇		T5	T7	T9	T11	T12	T14
Try this:	Reverse the lights and darks in every other block.							

Memory Blocks II

4-Unit Grid

Color Illustration: page 20

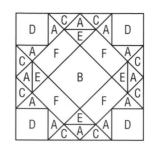

FOR 1 BLOCK:			**FINISHED BLOCK SIZE:** *Single dimensions in the cutting chart indicate the size of the cut square (3" = 3" x 3")*					
			4"	**6"**	**8"**	**9"**	**10"**	**12"**
Light	A: 3 ⊠→⊠		2¼"	2¾"	3¼"	3½"	3¾"	4¼"
	B: 1 ◇		T7	T11	T14	T15	T16	T19
Medium	C: 2 ⊠→⊠		2¼"	2¾"	3¼"	3½"	3¾"	4¼"
	D: 4 ☐		1½"	2"	2½"	2¾"	3"	3½"
Dark	E: 1 ⊠→⊠		2¼"	2¾"	3¼"	3½"	3¾"	4¼"
	F: 4 ◇		T32	T41	T51	T56	T59	T67

Try this: Use a medium- or large-scale print for B.

Midnight Sun

10-Unit Grid

Color Illustration: page 20

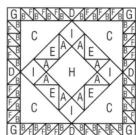

FOR 1 BLOCK:			**FINISHED BLOCK SIZE:** *Single dimensions in the cutting chart indicate the size of the cut square (3" = 3" x 3")*					
			6¼"	**7½"**	**8¾"**	**10"**	**12½"**	**13¾"**
Light	A: 2 ⊠→⊠		2½"	2¾"	3"	3¼"	3¾"	4"
	B: 16 ☐→◹		1½"	1⅝"	1¾"	1⅞"	2⅛"	2¼"
Dark	C: 2 ☐→◹		3⅜"	3⅞"	4⅜"	4⅞"	5⅞"	6⅜"
	D: 1 ⊠→⊠		2½"	2¾"	3"	3¼"	3¾"	4"
	E: 2 ☐→◹		2⅛"	2⅜"	2⅝"	2⅞"	3⅜"	3⅝"
	F: 12 ☐→◹		1½"	1⅝"	1¾"	1⅞"	2⅛"	2¼"
	G: 4 ☐		1⅛"	1¼"	1⅜"	1½"	1¾"	1⅞"
	H: 1 ◇		T9	T11	T12	T14	T16	T18
	I: 4 ◇		T4	T5	T6	T7	T9	T10

Try this: Use a medium instead of a dark for C.

☐ *Light* ▦ *Light 2* ▨ *Medium* ▨ *Medium 2* ■ *Dark*

Mill Wheel

4-Unit Grid
Color Illustration: page 20

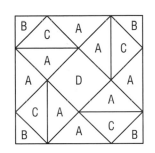

FOR 1 block:		**FINISHED BLOCK SIZE:** *Single dimensions in the cutting chart indicate the size of the cut square (3" = 3" x 3")*					
		4"	**6"**	**8"**	**9"**	**10"**	**12"**
Light	A: 2 ⊠→⊠	3¼"	4¼"	5¼"	5¾"	6¼"	7¼"
	B: 2 ◹→◨	1⅞"	2⅜"	2⅞"	3⅛"	3⅜"	3⅞"
Dark	C: 1 ⊠→⊠	3¼"	4¼"	5¼"	5¾"	6¼"	7¼"
	D: 1 ◇	T7	T11	T14	T15	T16	T19
Try this:		Use a medium instead of a light for the four "A" pieces that are part of the "wheel."					

Mineral Wells

8-Unit Grid
Color Illustration: page 20

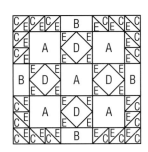

FOR 1 block:		**FINISHED BLOCK SIZE:** *Single dimensions in the cutting chart indicate the size of the cut square (3" = 3" x 3")*					
		6"	**8"**	**9"**	**10"**	**12"**	**14"**
Light	A: 5 ▢	2"	2½"	2¾"	3"	3½"	4"
	B: 4 ▭	1¼" x 2"	1½" x 2½"	1⅝" x 2¾"	1¾" x 3"	2" x 3½"	2¼" x 4"
	C: 10 ◹→◸	1⅝"	1⅞"	2"	2⅛"	2⅜"	2⅝"
	D: 4 ◇	T5	T7	T8	T9	T11	T12
Dark	E: 18 ◹→◥	1⅝"	1⅞"	2"	2⅛"	2⅜"	2⅝"
Try this:		Use one light for A and B and a different light for C and D.					

Missouri Star

4-Unit Grid

Color Illustration: page 20

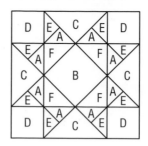

FOR 1 BLOCK:		FINISHED BLOCK SIZE: *Single dimensions in the cutting chart indicate the size of the cut square (3" = 3" x 3")*					
		4"	**6"**	**8"**	**9"**	**10"**	**12"**
Light	A: 2 ⊠→⊠	2¼"	2¾"	3¼"	3½"	3¾"	4¼"
	B: 1 ◇	T7	T11	T14	T15	T16	T19
Medium	C: 1 ⊠→⊠	3¼"	4¼"	5¼"	5¾"	6¼"	7¼"
	D: 4 □	1½"	2"	2½"	2¾"	3"	3½"
Dark	E: 2 ⊠→⊠	2¼"	2¾"	3¼"	3½"	3¾"	4¼"
	F: 2 ◻→◻	1⅞"	2⅜"	2⅞"	3⅛"	3⅜"	3⅞"
Try this:		Reverse the mediums and darks in every other block.					

Mosaic

6-Unit Grid

Color Illustration: page 20

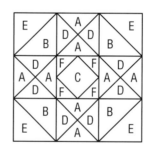

FOR 1 BLOCK:		FINISHED BLOCK SIZE: *Single dimensions in the cutting chart indicate the size of the cut square (3" = 3" x 3")*					
		4½"	**6"**	**7½"**	**9"**	**10½"**	**12"**
Light	A: 2 ⊠→⊠	2¾"	3¼"	3¾"	4¼"	4¾"	5¼"
	B: 2 ◻→◻	2⅜"	2⅞"	3⅜"	3⅞"	4⅜"	4⅞"
	C: 1 ◇	T5	T7	T9	T11	T12	T14
Dark	D: 2 ⊠→⊠	2¾"	3¼"	3¾"	4¼"	4¾"	5¼"
	E: 2 ◻→◻	2⅜"	2⅞"	3⅜"	3⅞"	4⅜"	4⅞"
	F: 2 ◻→◻	1⅝"	1⅞"	2⅛"	2⅜"	2⅝"	2⅞"
Try this:		Use a medium instead of a dark for E and F.					

88   □ *Light*   ▧ *Light 2*   ▨ *Medium*   ▦ *Medium 2*   ■ *Dark*

Mosaic #3

4-Unit Grid

Color Illustration: page 20

 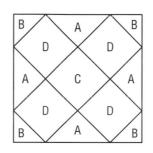

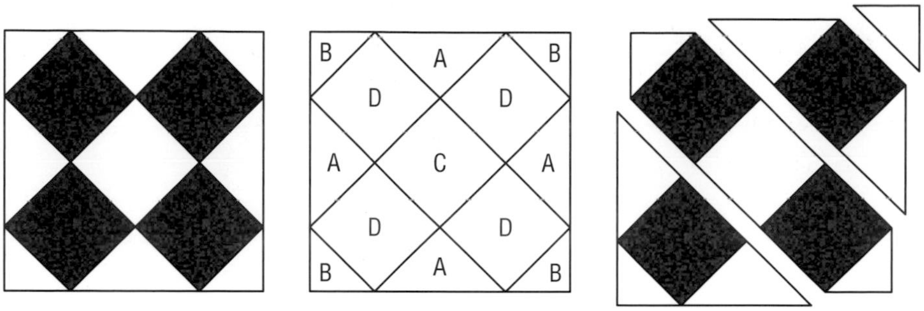

		FINISHED BLOCK SIZE: Single dimensions in the cutting chart indicate the size of the cut square (3" = 3" x 3")					
FOR 1 BLOCK:		**4"**	**6"**	**8"**	**9"**	**10"**	**12"**
Light	A: 1	3¼"	4¼"	5¼"	5¾"	6¼"	7¼"
	B: 2	1⅞"	2⅜"	2⅞"	3⅛"	3⅜"	3⅞"
	C: 1	T7	T11	T14	T15	T16	T19
Dark	D: 4	T7	T11	T14	T15	T16	T19
Try this:	Use several different darks for D.						

Mosaic #10

4-Unit Grid

Color Illustration: page 20

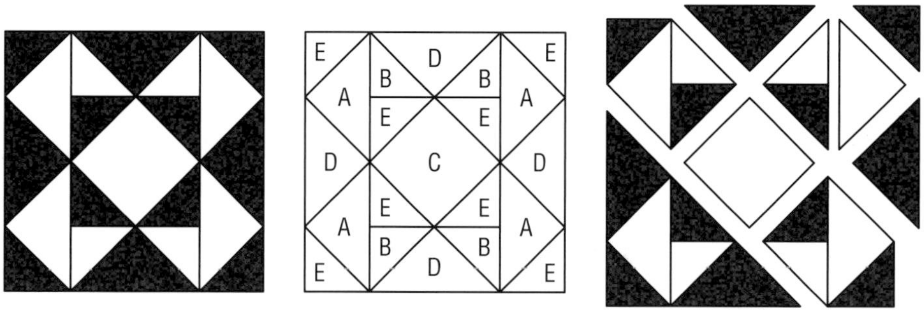

		FINISHED BLOCK SIZE: Single dimensions in the cutting chart indicate the size of the cut square (3" = 3" x 3")					
FOR 1 BLOCK:		**4"**	**6"**	**8"**	**9"**	**10"**	**12"**
Light	A: 1	3¼"	4¼"	5¼"	5¾"	6¼"	7¼"
	B: 2	1⅞"	2⅜"	2⅞"	3⅛"	3⅜"	3⅞"
	C: 1	T7	T11	T14	T15	T16	T19
Dark	D: 1	3¼"	4¼"	5¼"	5¾"	6¼"	7¼"
	E: 4	1⅞"	2⅜"	2⅞"	3⅛"	3⅜"	3⅞"
Try this:	Use a light and a medium instead of a light and a dark in every other block.						

Mosaic #19

4-Unit Grid

Color Illustration: page 20

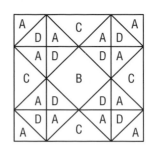

			FINISHED BLOCK SIZE: *Single dimensions in the cutting chart indicate the size of the cut square (3" = 3" x 3")*					
FOR 1 BLOCK:			**4"**	**6"**	**8"**	**9"**	**10"**	**12"**
Light	A: 6		1⅞"	2⅜"	2⅞"	3⅛"	3⅜"	3⅞"
	B: 1		T7	T11	T14	T15	T16	T19
Dark	C: 1		3¼"	4¼"	5¼"	5¾"	6¼"	7¼"
	D: 4		1⅞"	2⅜"	2⅞"	3⅛"	3⅜"	3⅞"
Try this:		Reverse the lights and darks.						

Mosaic #21

4-Unit Grid

Color Illustration: page 20

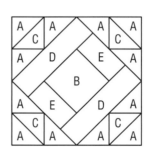

			FINISHED BLOCK SIZE: *Single dimensions in the cutting chart indicate the size of the cut square (3" = 3" x 3")*					
FOR 1 BLOCK:			**4"**	**6"**	**8"**	**9"**	**10"**	**12"**
Light	A: 6		1⅞"	2⅜"	2⅞"	3⅛"	3⅜"	3⅞"
	B: 1		T7	T11	T14	T15	T16	T19
Dark	C: 2		1⅞"	2⅜"	2⅞"	3⅛"	3⅜"	3⅞"
	D: 2		T34	T43	T53	T58	T61	T69
	E: 2		T32	T41	T51	T56	T59	T67
Try this:		Use one light for A and a different light or a medium for B.						

□ Light ▨ Light 2 ▨ Medium ▨ Medium 2 ■ Dark

Mosaic #22

4-Unit Grid

Color Illustration: page 20

 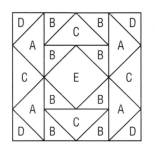 

FOR 1 BLOCK:			FINISHED BLOCK SIZE: *Single dimensions in the cutting chart indicate the size of the cut square (3" = 3" x 3")*					
			4"	**6"**	**8"**	**9"**	**10"**	**12"**
Light	A: 1	⊠→⊠	3¼"	4¼"	5¼"	5¾"	6¼"	7¼"
	B: 4	◺→◹	1⅞"	2⅜"	2⅞"	3⅛"	3⅜"	3⅞"
Dark	C: 1	⊠→⊠	3¼"	4¼"	5¼"	5¾"	6¼"	7¼"
	D: 2	◺→◹	1⅞"	2⅜"	2⅞"	3⅛"	3⅜"	3⅞"
	E: 1	◇	T7	T11	T14	T15	T16	T19
Try this:		Use a medium instead of a light for A.						

Mosaic Rose

6-Unit Grid

Color Illustration: page 21

 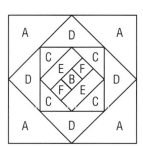 

FOR 1 BLOCK:			FINISHED BLOCK SIZE: *Single dimensions in the cutting chart indicate the size of the cut square (3" = 3" x 3")*					
			4½"	**6"**	**7½"**	**9"**	**10½"**	**12"**
Light	A: 2	◺→◹	3⅛"	3⅞"	4⅝"	5⅜"	6⅛"	6⅞"
	B: 1	◇	T1	T2	T4	T5	T6	T7
Light 2	C: 2	◺→◹	2"	2⅜"	2¾"	3⅛"	3½"	3⅞"
Medium	D: 1	⊠→⊠	3½"	4¼"	5"	5¾"	6½"	7¼"
Dark	E: 2	◹	T29	T33	T37	T42	T47	T52
	F: 2	◇	T1	T2	T4	T5	T6	T7
Try this:		Reverse the medium and dark in every other block.						

Mrs. Brown's Choice

6-Unit Grid
Color Illustration: page 21

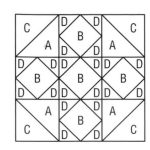

		FINISHED BLOCK SIZE:					
		Single dimensions in the cutting chart indicate the size of the cut square (3" = 3" x 3")					
FOR 1 BLOCK:		4½"	6"	7½"	9"	10½"	12"
Light	A: 2	2⅜"	2⅞"	3⅜"	3⅞"	4⅜"	4⅞"
	B: 5	T5	T7	T9	T11	T12	T14
Dark	C: 2	2⅜"	2⅞"	3⅜"	3⅞"	4⅜"	4⅞"
	D: 10	1⅝"	1⅞"	2⅛"	2⅜"	2⅝"	2⅞"
Try this:	Use one dark for C and a different dark for D.						

New Album

4-Unit Grid
Color Illustration: page 21

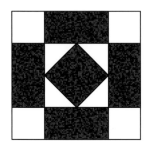
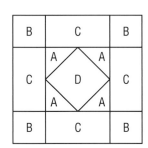
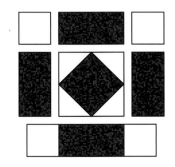

		FINISHED BLOCK SIZE:					
		Single dimensions in the cutting chart indicate the size of the cut square (3" = 3" x 3")					
FOR 1 BLOCK:		4"	6"	8"	9"	10"	12"
Light	A: 2	1⅞"	2⅜"	2⅞"	3⅛"	3⅜"	3⅞"
	B: 4	1½"	2"	2½"	2¾"	3"	3½"
Dark	C: 4	1½" x 2½"	2" x 3½"	2½" x 4½"	2¾" x 5"	3" x 5½"	3½" x 6½"
	D: 1	T7	T11	T14	T15	T16	T19
Try this:	Use a medium instead of a dark for D.						

☐ Light   ▦ Light 2   ▩ Medium   ▨ Medium 2   ■ Dark

New Hampshire's Granite Rock

6-Unit Grid

Color Illustration: page 21

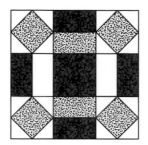

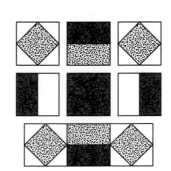

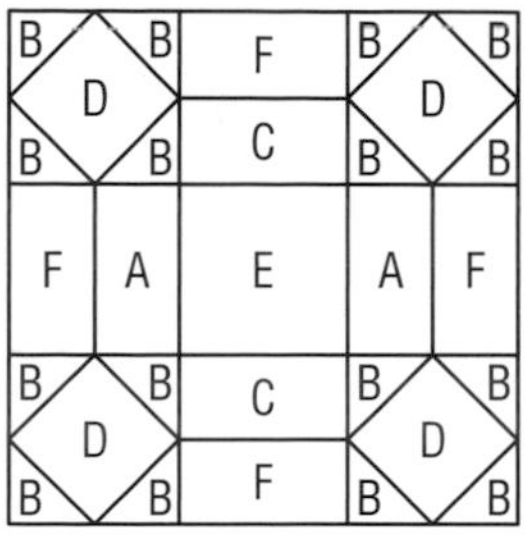

			FINISHED BLOCK SIZE: *Single dimensions in the cutting chart indicate the size of the cut square (3" = 3" x 3")*					
FOR 1 BLOCK:			**4½"**	**6"**	**7½"**	**9"**	**10½"**	**12"**
Light	A: 2		1¼" x 2"	1½" x 2½"	1¾" x 3"	2" x 3½"	2¼" x 4"	2½" x 4½"
	B: 8		1⅝"	1⅞"	2⅛"	2⅜"	2⅝"	2⅞"
Medium	C: 2		1¼" x 2"	1½" x 2½"	1¾" x 3"	2" x 3½"	2¼" x 4"	2½" x 4½"
	D: 4		T5	T7	T9	T11	T12	T14
Dark	E: 1		2"	2½"	3"	3½"	4"	4½"
	F: 4		1¼" x 2"	1½" x 2½"	1¾" x 3"	2" x 3½"	2¼" x 4"	2½" x 4½"
Try this:	Reverse the lights and darks in every other block.							

New Hour Glass

6-Unit Grid

Color Illustration: page 21

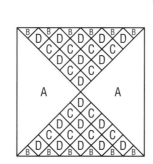

			FINISHED BLOCK SIZE: *Single dimensions in the cutting chart indicate the size of the cut square (3" = 3" x 3")*					
FOR 2 BLOCKS:			**4½"**	**6"**	**7½"**	**9"**	**10½"**	**12"**
Light	A: 1		5¾"	7¼"	8¾"	10¼"	11¾"	13¼"
	B: 6		2"	2¼"	2½"	2¾"	3"	3¼"
	C: 24		T1	T2	T4	T5	T6	T7
Dark	D: 36		T1	T2	T4	T5	T6	T7
Try this:	Use many different darks for D.							

93

Nine Patch Checkerboard

6-Unit Grid

Color Illustration: page 21

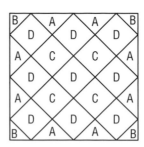

FOR 1 BLOCK:		FINISHED BLOCK SIZE: Single dimensions in the cutting chart indicate the size of the cut square (3" = 3" x 3")					
		4½"	6"	7½"	9"	10½"	12"
Light	A: 2 ⊠ → ⊠	2¾"	3¼"	3¾"	4¼"	4¾"	5¼"
	B: 2 ◺ → ◺	1⅝"	1⅞"	2⅛"	2⅜"	2⅝"	2⅞"
	C: 4 ◇	T5	T7	T9	T11	T12	T14
Dark	D: 9 ◇	T5	T7	T9	T11	T12	T14
Try this:	Reverse the lights and darks in every other block.						

Northumber-land Star

4-Unit Grid

Color Illustration: page 21

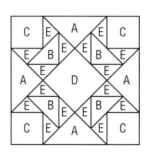

FOR 1 BLOCK:		FINISHED BLOCK SIZE: Single dimensions in the cutting chart indicate the size of the cut square (3" = 3" x 3")					
		4"	6"	8"	9"	10"	12"
Light	A: 1 ⊠ → ⊠	3¼"	4¼"	5¼"	5¾"	6¼"	7¼"
	B: 2 ◺ → ◺	1⅞"	2⅜"	2⅞"	3⅛"	3⅜"	3⅞"
	C: 4 ☐	1½"	2"	2½"	2¾"	3"	3½"
Medium	D: 1 ◇	T7	T11	T14	T15	T16	T19
Dark	E: 4 ⊠ → ⊠	2¼"	2¾"	3¼"	3½"	3¾"	4¼"
Try this:	Use one light for A and C and a different light for B.						

☐ *Light* ░ *Light 2* ▨ *Medium* ▓ *Medium 2* ■ *Dark*

Odd Fellows

5-Unit Grid

Color Illustration: page 21

 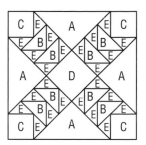 

FOR 1 BLOCK:			FINISHED BLOCK SIZE: *Single dimensions in the cutting chart indicate the size of the cut square (3" = 3" x 3")*					
			5"	**6¼"**	**7½"**	**8¾"**	**10"**	**12½"**
Light	A: 1		4¼"	5"	5¾"	6½"	7¼"	8¾"
	B: 4		1⅞"	2⅛"	2⅜"	2⅝"	2⅞"	3⅜"
	C: 4		1½"	1¾"	2"	2¼"	2½"	3"
	D: 1		T7	T9	T11	T12	T14	T16
Dark	E: 6		2¼"	2½"	2¾"	3"	3¼"	3¾"

Try this: Use several different lights for B.

Odd Fellow's Cross

5-Unit Grid

Color Illustration: page 21

 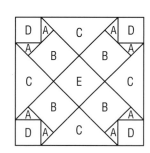 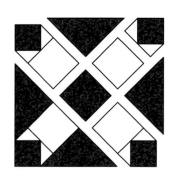

FOR 1 BLOCK:			FINISHED BLOCK SIZE: *Single dimensions in the cutting chart indicate the size of the cut square (3" = 3" x 3")*					
			5"	**6¼"**	**7½"**	**8¾"**	**10"**	**12½"**
Light	A: 2		2¼"	2½"	2¾"	3"	3¼"	3¾"
	B: 4		T7	T9	T11	T12	T14	T16
Dark	C: 1		4¼"	5"	5¾"	6½"	7¼"	8¾"
	D: 4		1½"	1¾"	2"	2¼"	2½"	3"
	E: 1		T7	T9	T11	T12	T14	T16

Try this: Use a medium instead of a dark for C.

The Old Rugged Cross

6-Unit Grid

Color Illustration: page 21

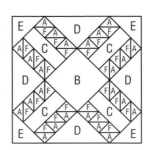

FOR 1 BLOCK:			FINISHED BLOCK SIZE: *Single dimensions in the cutting chart indicate the size of the cut square (3" = 3" x 3")*					
			4½"	6"	7½"	9"	10½"	12"
Light	A: 6		2"	2¼"	2½"	2¾"	3"	3¼"
	B: 1		T8	T11	T13	T15	T17	T19
	C: 4		T29	T33	T37	T42	T47	T52
Medium	D: 1		3½"	4¼"	5"	5¾"	6½"	7¼"
	E: 2		2"	2⅜"	2¾"	3⅛"	3½"	3⅞"
Dark	F: 6		2"	2¼"	2½"	2¾"	3"	3¼"
Try this:	Reverse the mediums and darks in every other block.							

Old Time Block

6-Unit Grid

Color Illustration: page 21

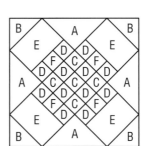

FOR 1 BLOCK:			FINISHED BLOCK SIZE: *Single dimensions in the cutting chart indicate the size of the cut square (3" = 3" x 3")*					
			4½"	6"	7½"	9"	10½"	12"
Light	A: 1		3½"	4¼"	5"	5¾"	6½"	7¼"
	B: 2		2"	2⅜"	2¾"	3⅛"	3½"	3⅞"
	C: 5		T1	T2	T4	T5	T6	T7
Medium	D: 12		T1	T2	T4	T5	T6	T7
Dark	E: 4		T77	T78	T79	T80	T81	T82
	F: 4		T1	T2	T4	T5	T6	T7
Try this:	Use several different mediums for D.							

☐ Light   ⠿ Light 2   ▨ Medium   ▩ Medium 2   ■ Dark

An Original Design

6-Unit Grid

Color Illustration: page 21

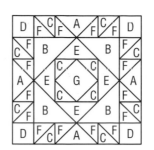

FOR 1 BLOCK:			FINISHED BLOCK SIZE: *Single dimensions in the cutting chart indicate the size of the cut square (3" = 3" x 3")*					
			4½"	6"	7½"	9"	10½"	12"
Light	A: 1 ⊠→⊠		2¾"	3¼"	3¾"	4¼"	4¾"	5¼"
	B: 2 ◺→◺		2⅜"	2⅞"	3⅜"	3⅞"	4⅜"	4⅞"
	C: 6 ◺→◺		1⅝"	1⅞"	2⅛"	2⅜"	2⅝"	2⅞"
	D: 4 ▢		1¼"	1½"	1¾"	2"	2¼"	2½"
Dark	E: 1 ⊠→⊠		2¾"	3¼"	3¾"	4¼"	4¾"	5¼"
	F: 8 ◺→◺		1⅝"	1⅞"	2⅛"	2⅜"	2⅝"	2⅞"
	G: 1 ◇		T5	T7	T9	T11	T12	T14
Try this:	Use a medium instead of a dark for E.							

Pattern Without a Name

3-Unit Grid

Color Illustration: page 22

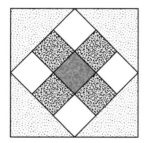
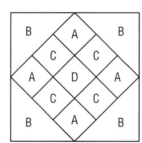
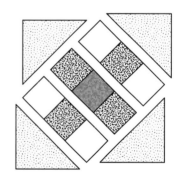

FOR 1 BLOCK:			FINISHED BLOCK SIZE: *Single dimensions in the cutting chart indicate the size of the cut square (3" = 3" x 3")*					
			4½"	6"	7½"	9"	10½"	12"
Light	A: 4 ◇		T5	T7	T9	T11	T12	T14
Light 2	B: 2 ◺→◺		3⅛"	3⅞"	4⅝"	5⅜"	6⅛"	6⅞"
Medium	C: 4 ◇		T5	T7	T9	T11	T12	T14
Medium 2	D: 1 ◇		T5	T7	T9	T11	T12	T14
Try this:	Use a different combination of fabrics in every block.							

Pavement Pattern

4-Unit Grid

Color Illustration: page 22

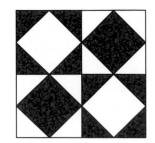

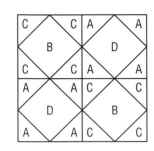

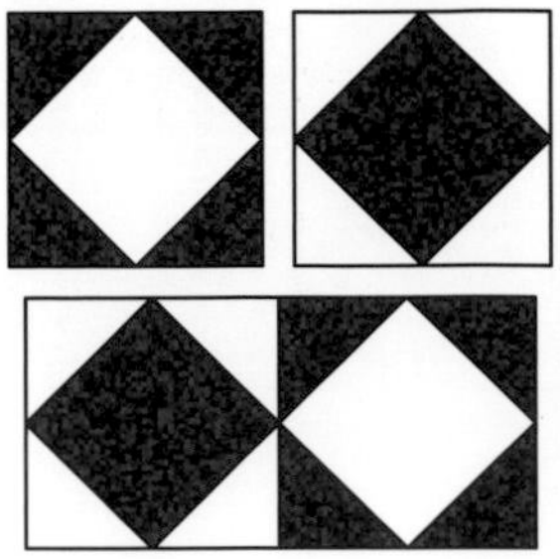

			FINISHED BLOCK SIZE: *Single dimensions in the cutting chart indicate the size of the cut square (3" = 3" x 3")*					
FOR 1 BLOCK:			**4"**	**6"**	**8"**	**9"**	**10"**	**12"**
Light	A: 4		1⅞"	2⅜"	2⅞"	3⅛"	3⅜"	3⅞"
	B: 2		T7	T11	T14	T15	T16	T19
Dark	C: 4		1⅞"	2⅜"	2⅞"	3⅛"	3⅜"	3⅞"
	D: 2		T7	T11	T14	T15	T16	T19
Try this:		Use a different combination of lights and darks in each quadrant of the block.						

Pershing

6-Unit Grid

Color Illustration: page 22

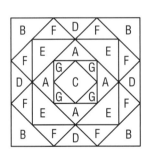

			FINISHED BLOCK SIZE: *Single dimensions in the cutting chart indicate the size of the cut square (3" = 3" x 3")*					
FOR 1 BLOCK:			**4½"**	**6"**	**7½"**	**9"**	**10½"**	**12"**
Light	A: 1		2¾"	3¼"	3¾"	4¼"	4¾"	5¼"
	B: 2		2⅜"	2⅞"	3⅜"	3⅞"	4⅜"	4⅞"
	C: 1		T5	T7	T9	T11	T12	T14
Medium	D: 1		2¾"	3¼"	3¾"	4¼"	4¾"	5¼"
	E: 2		2⅜"	2⅞"	3⅜"	3⅞"	4⅜"	4⅞"
Medium 2	F: 2		2¾"	3¼"	3¾"	4¼"	4¾"	5¼"
Dark	G: 2		1⅝"	1⅞"	2⅛"	2⅜"	2⅝"	2⅞"
Try this:		Use a light instead of a medium for D.						

☐ *Light*   ▦ *Light 2*   ▨ *Medium*   ▧ *Medium 2*   ■ *Dark*

Pyramids

4-Unit Grid

Color Illustration: page 22

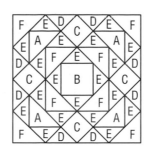

FOR 1 BLOCK:		FINISHED BLOCK SIZE: Single dimensions in the cutting chart indicate the size of the cut square (3" = 3" x 3")					
		4"	**6"**	**8"**	**9"**	**10"**	**12"**
Light	A: 2 ▢→◪	1⅞"	2⅜"	2⅞"	3⅛"	3⅜"	3⅞"
	B: 1 ▢	1½"	2"	2½"	2¾"	3"	3½"
	C: 4 ◇	T2	T5	T7	T8	T9	T11
Light 2	D: 2 ⊠→⊠	2¼"	2¾"	3¼"	3½"	3¾"	4¼"
Medium	E: 5 ⊠→⊠	2¼"	2¾"	3¼"	3½"	3¾"	4¼"
Dark	F: 4 ▢→◪	1⅞"	2⅜"	2⅞"	3⅛"	3⅜"	3⅞"
Try this:	Reverse the mediums and darks.						

Quilt in Light and Dark

4-Unit Grid

Color Illustration: page 22

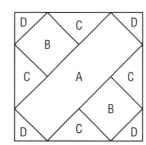

FOR 1 BLOCK:		FINISHED BLOCK SIZE: Single dimensions in the cutting chart indicate the size of the cut square (3" = 3" x 3")					
		4"	**6"**	**8"**	**9"**	**10"**	**12"**
Light	A: 1 ◇	T52	T68	T73	T74	T75	T76
	B: 2 ◇	T7	T11	T14	T15	T16	T19
Dark	C: 1 ⊠→⊠	3¼"	4¼"	5¼"	5¾"	6¼"	7¼"
	D: 2 ▢→◪	1⅞"	2⅜"	2⅞"	3⅛"	3⅜"	3⅞"
Try this:	Reverse the lights and darks in every other block.						

Red Cross

8-Unit Grid

Color Illustration: page 22

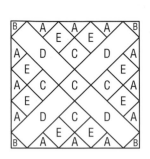

FOR 1 BLOCK:		FINISHED BLOCK SIZE: *Single dimensions in the cutting chart indicate the size of the cut square (3" = 3" x 3")*					
		6"	8"	9"	10"	12"	14"
Light	A: 3 ⊠→⊠	2¾"	3¼"	3½"	3¾"	4¼"	4¾"
	B: 2 ◻→◻	1⅝"	1⅞"	2"	2⅛"	2⅜"	2⅝"
	C: 5 ◇	T5	T7	T8	T9	T11	T12
Dark	D: 4 ◇	T42	T52	T57	T60	T68	T71
	E: 8 ◇	T5	T7	T8	T9	T11	T12

Try this: Use one light for A and B and a different light for C.

Reverse X

8-Unit Grid

Color Illustration: page 22

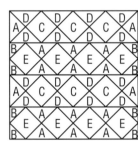

FOR 1 BLOCK:		FINISHED BLOCK SIZE: *Single dimensions in the cutting chart indicate the size of the cut square (3" = 3" x 3")*					
		6"	8"	9"	10"	12"	14"
Light	A: 4 ⊠→⊠	2¾"	3¼"	3½"	3¾"	4¼"	4¾"
	B: 4 ◻→◻	1⅝"	1⅞"	2"	2⅛"	2⅜"	2⅝"
	C: 6 ◇	T5	T7	T8	T9	T11	T12
Dark	D: 4 ⊠→⊠	2¾"	3¼"	3½"	3¾"	4¼"	4¾"
	E: 8 ◇	T5	T7	T8	T9	T11	T12

Try this: Use many different lights and darks.

◻ Light ⬚ Light 2 ▦ Medium ▨ Medium 2 ■ Dark

Rhode Island

6-Unit Grid

Color Illustration: page 22

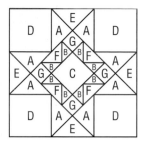

FOR 1 BLOCK:			FINISHED BLOCK SIZE: *Single dimensions in the cutting chart indicate the size of the cut square (3" = 3" x 3")*					
			4½"	6"	7½"	9"	10½"	12"
Light	A: 2		2¾"	3¼"	3¾"	4¼"	4¾"	5¼"
	B: 2		2"	2¼"	2½"	2¾"	3"	3¼"
	C: 1		T5	T7	T9	T11	T12	T14
Medium	D: 4		2"	2½"	3"	3½"	4"	4½"
Dark	E: 1		2¾"	3¼"	3¾"	4¼"	4¾"	5¼"
	F: 2		1⅝"	1⅞"	2⅛"	2⅜"	2⅝"	2⅞"
	G: 4		T1	T2	T4	T5	T6	T7
Try this:		Use one light for A and a different light for B and C.						

Richmond

6-Unit Grid

Color Illustration: page 22

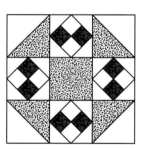
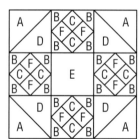

FOR 1 BLOCK:			FINISHED BLOCK SIZE: *Single dimensions in the cutting chart indicate the size of the cut square (3" = 3" x 3")*					
			4½"	6"	7½"	9"	10½"	12"
Light	A: 2		2⅜"	2⅞"	3⅜"	3⅞"	4⅜"	4⅞"
	B: 8		1⅝"	1⅞"	2⅛"	2⅜"	2⅝"	2⅞"
	C: 8		T1	T2	T4	T5	T6	T7
Medium	D: 2		2⅜"	2⅞"	3⅜"	3⅞"	4⅜"	4⅞"
	E: 1		2"	2½"	3"	3½"	4"	4½"
Dark	F: 8		T1	T2	T4	T5	T6	T7
Try this:		Reverse the mediums and darks in every other block.						

Right and Left

2-Unit Grid

Color Illustration: page 22

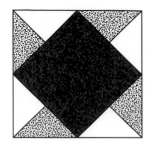
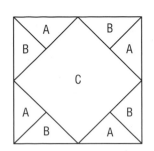

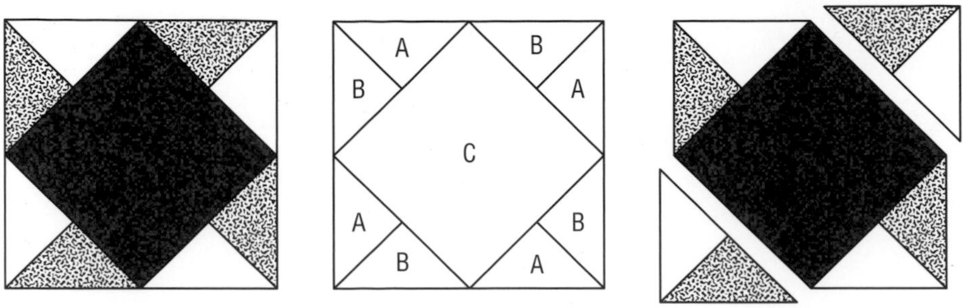

		FINISHED BLOCK SIZE *Single dimensions in the cutting chart indicate the size of the cut square (3" = 3" x 3")*					
FOR 1 BLOCK:		**4"**	**6"**	**8"**	**9"**	**10"**	**12"**
Light	A: 1 ⊠→⊠	3¼"	4¼"	5¼"	5¾"	6¼"	7¼"
Medium	B: 1 ⊠→⊠	3¼"	4¼"	5¼"	5¾"	6¼"	7¼"
Dark	C: 1 ◇	T14	T19	T23	T24	T25	T27
Try this:	Use a large-scale print for C.						

Rocky Glen II

10-Unit Grid

Color Illustration: page 22

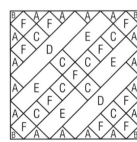
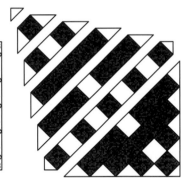

		FINISHED BLOCK SIZE: *Single dimensions in the cutting chart indicate the size of the cut square (3" = 3" x 3")*					
FOR 1 BLOCK:		**6¼"**	**7½"**	**8¾"**	**10"**	**12½"**	**13¾"**
Light	A: 4 ⊠→⊠	2½"	2¾"	3"	3¼"	3¾"	4"
	B: 2 ◻→◻	1½"	1⅝"	1¾"	1⅞"	2⅛"	2¼"
	C: 8 ◇	T4	T5	T6	T7	T9	T10
Dark	D: 2 ◇	T39	T44	T49	T54	T62	T66
	E: 4 ◇	T37	T42	T47	T52	T60	T64
	F: 11 ◇	T4	T5	T6	T7	T9	T10
Try this:	Use a different combination of lights and darks in every block.						

 Light   *Light 2*   *Medium*   *Medium 2*  *Dark*

Rocky Mountain Chain

10-Unit Grid

Color Illustration: page 22

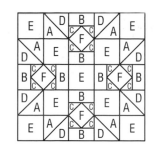

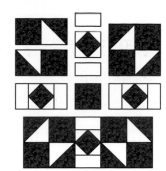

			FINISHED BLOCK SIZE:				
			Single dimensions in the cutting chart indicate the size of the cut square (3" = 3" x 3")				
FOR 1 BLOCK:			**6¼"**	**7½"**	**8¾"**	**10"**	**12½"**	**13¾"**
Light	A: 4		2⅛"	2⅜"	2⅝"	2⅞"	3⅜"	3⅝"
	B: 8		1⅛" x 1¾"	1¼" x 2"	1⅜" x 2¼"	1½" x 2½"	1¾" x 3"	1⅞" x 3¼"
	C: 8		1½"	1⅝"	1¾"	1⅞"	2⅛"	2¼"
Dark	D: 4		2⅛"	2⅜"	2⅝"	2⅞"	3⅜"	3⅝"
	E: 9		1¾"	2"	2¼"	2½"	3"	3¼"
	F: 4		T4	T5	T6	T7	T9	T10
Try this:		Use a medium instead of a light for C.						

Rolling Squares

6-Unit Grid

Color Illustration: page 23

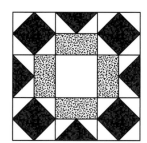

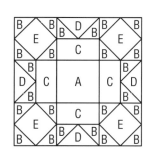

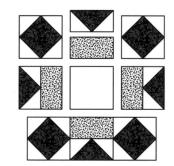

			FINISHED BLOCK SIZE:				
			Single dimensions in the cutting chart indicate the size of the cut square (3" = 3" x 3")				
FOR 1 BLOCK:			**4½"**	**6"**	**7½"**	**9"**	**10½"**	**12"**
Light	A: 1		2"	2½"	3"	3½"	4"	4½"
	B: 12		1⅝"	1⅞"	2⅛"	2⅜"	2⅝"	2⅞"
Medium	C: 4		1¼" x 2"	1½" x 2½"	1¾" x 3"	2" x 3½"	2¼" x 4"	2½" x 4½"
Dark	D: 1		2¾"	3¼"	3¾"	4¼"	4¾"	5¼"
	E: 4		T5	T7	T9	T11	T12	T14
Try this:		Reverse the mediums and darks.						

Rolling Stone

6-Unit Grid

Color Illustration: page 23

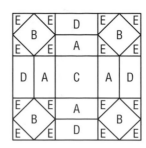

FOR 1 BLOCK:			FINISHED BLOCK SIZE: *Single dimensions in the cutting chart indicate the size of the cut square (3" = 3" x 3")*					
			4½"	6"	7½"	9"	10½"	12"
Light	A: 4 ▭		1¼" x 2"	1½" x 2½"	1¾" x 3"	2" x 3½"	2¼" x 4"	2½" x 4½"
	B: 4 ◇		T5	T7	T9	T11	T12	T14
Dark	C: 1 ▢		2"	2½"	3"	3½"	4"	4½"
	D: 4 ▭		1¼" x 2"	1½" x 2½"	1¾" x 3"	2" x 3½"	2¼" x 4"	2½" x 4½"
	E: 8 ◺→◺		1⅝"	1⅞"	2⅛"	2⅜"	2⅝"	2⅞"
Try this:		Reverse the lights and darks in every other block.						

Roman Cross

8-Unit Grid

Color Illustration: page 23

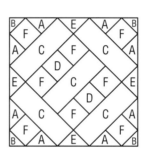

FOR 1 BLOCK:			FINISHED BLOCK SIZE: *Single dimensions in the cutting chart indicate the size of the cut square (3" = 3" x 3")*					
			6"	8"	9"	10"	12"	14"
Light	A: 2 ⊠→⊠		2¾"	3¼"	3½"	3¾"	4¼"	4¾"
	B: 2 ◺→◺		1⅝"	1⅞"	2"	2⅛"	2⅜"	2⅝"
	C: 5 ◇		T42	T52	T57	T60	T68	T71
	D: 2 ◇		T5	T7	T8	T9	T11	T12
Dark	E: 1 ⊠→⊠		2¾"	3¼"	3½"	3¾"	4¼"	4¾"
	F: 8 ◇		T5	T7	T8	T9	T11	T12
Try this:		Use several different darks for F.						

☐ *Light*   ▦ *Light 2*   ▨ *Medium*   ▨ *Medium 2*   ■ *Dark*

St. John Pavement

5-Unit Grid

Color Illustration: page 23

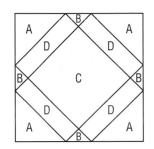

FOR 1 BLOCK:			FINISHED BLOCK SIZE: *Single dimensions in the cutting chart indicate the size of the cut square (3" = 3" x 3")*					
			5"	6¼"	7½"	8¾"	10"	12½"
Light	A: 2		2⅞"	3⅜"	3⅞"	4⅜"	4⅞"	5⅞"
	B: 1		2¼"	2½"	2¾"	3"	3¼"	3¾"
	C: 1		T14	T16	T19	T21	T23	T25
Dark	D: 4		T34	T38	T43	T48	T53	T61
Try this:		Use a medium- or large-scale print for C.						

Sally's Favorite

4-Unit Grid

Color Illustration: page 23

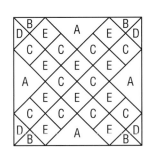

FOR 1 BLOCK:			FINISHED BLOCK SIZE: *Single dimensions in the cutting chart indicate the size of the cut square (3" = 3" x 3")*					
			4"	6"	8"	9"	10"	12"
Light	A: 1		3¼"	4¼"	5¼"	5¾"	6¼"	7¼"
	B: 1		2¼"	2¾"	3¼"	3½"	3¾"	4¼"
	C: 10		T2	T5	T7	T8	T9	T11
Dark	D: 1		2¼"	2¾"	3¼"	3½"	3¾"	4¼"
	E: 10		T2	T5	T7	T8	T9	T11
Try this:		Use a medium instead of a light for A.						

Salt Lake City

4-Unit Grid

Color Illustration: page 23

 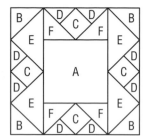 

FOR 1 BLOCK:		FINISHED BLOCK SIZE: *Single dimensions in the cutting chart indicate the size of the cut square (3" = 3" x 3")*					
		4"	**6"**	**8"**	**9"**	**10"**	**12"**
Light	A: 1	2½"	3½"	4½"	5"	5½"	6½"
	B: 2	1⅞"	2⅜"	2⅞"	3⅛"	3⅜"	3⅞"
	C: 4	T2	T5	T7	T8	T9	T11
Medium	D: 2	2¼"	2¾"	3¼"	3½"	3¾"	4¼"
Dark	E: 1	3¼"	4¼"	5¼"	5¾"	6¼"	7¼"
	F: 2	1⅞"	2⅜"	2⅞"	3⅛"	3⅜"	3⅞"
Try this:		Use one light for A and C and a different light for B.					

A Salute to the Colors

4-Unit Grid

Color Illustration: page 23

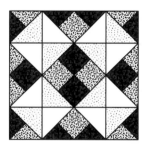 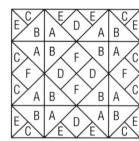 

FOR 1 BLOCK:		FINISHED BLOCK SIZE: *Single dimensions in the cutting chart indicate the size of the cut square (3" = 3" x 3")*					
		4"	**6"**	**8"**	**9"**	**10"**	**12"**
Light	A: 4	1⅞"	2⅜"	2⅞"	3⅛"	3⅜"	3⅞"
Light 2	B: 4	1⅞"	2⅜"	2⅞"	3⅛"	3⅜"	3⅞"
Medium	C: 2	2¼"	2¾"	3¼"	3½"	3¾"	4¼"
	D: 4	T2	T5	T7	T8	T9	T11
Dark	E: 2	2¼"	2¾"	3¼"	3½"	3¾"	4¼"
	F: 4	T2	T5	T7	T8	T9	T11
Try this:		Use a different combination of fabrics in every block.					

| Light | Light 2 | Medium | Medium 2 | Dark |

Scotch Squares

4-Unit Grid

Color Illustration: page 23

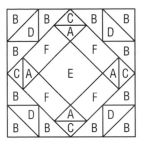

FOR 1 BLOCK:			FINISHED BLOCK SIZE: *Single dimensions in the cutting chart indicate the size of the cut square (3" = 3" x 3")*					
			4"	**6"**	**8"**	**9"**	**10"**	**12"**
Light	A: 1	⊠→⊠	2¼"	2¾"	3¼"	3½"	3¾"	4¼"
	B: 6	◻→◺	1⅞"	2⅜"	2⅞"	3⅛"	3⅜"	3⅞"
Medium	C: 1	⊠→⊠	2¼"	2¾"	3¼"	3½"	3¾"	4¼"
	D: 2	◻→◺	1⅞"	2⅜"	2⅞"	3⅛"	3⅜"	3⅞"
	E: 1	◇	T7	T11	T14	T15	T16	T19
Dark	F: 4	▱	T32	T41	T51	T56	T59	T67
Try this:		Reverse the lights and mediums in every other block.						

Snail's Trail II

8-Unit Grid

Color Illustration: page 23

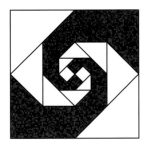
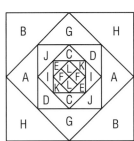

FOR 2 BLOCKS:			FINISHED BLOCK SIZE: *Single dimensions in the cutting chart indicate the size of the cut square (3" = 3" x 3")*					
			6"	**8"**	**9"**	**10"**	**12"**	**14"**
Light	A: 1	⊠→⊠	4¼"	5¼"	5¾"	6¼"	7¼"	8¼"
	B: 2	◻→◺	3⅞"	4⅞"	5⅜"	5⅞"	6⅞"	7⅞"
	C: 1	⊠→⊠	2¾"	3¼"	3½"	3¾"	4¼"	4¾"
	D: 2	◻→◺	2⅜"	2⅞"	3⅛"	3⅜"	3⅞"	4⅜"
	E: 2	◻→◺	1⅝"	1⅞"	2"	2⅛"	2⅜"	2⅝"
	F: 4	◇	T1	T2	T3	T4	T5	T6
Dark	G: 1	⊠→⊠	4¼"	5¼"	5¾"	6¼"	7¼"	8¼"
	H: 2	◻→◺	3⅞"	4⅞"	5⅜"	5⅞"	6⅞"	7⅞"
	I: 1	⊠→⊠	2¾"	3¼"	3½"	3¾"	4¼"	4¾"
	J: 2	◻→◺	2⅜"	2⅞"	3⅛"	3⅜"	3⅞"	4⅜"
	K: 2	◻→◺	1⅝"	1⅞"	2"	2⅛"	2⅜"	2⅝"
	L: 4	◇	T1	T2	T3	T4	T5	T6
Try this:		Use a light and a medium instead of a light and a dark.						

Spring Has Come

8-Unit Grid

Color Illustration: page 23

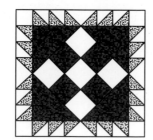
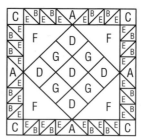

FOR 1 BLOCK:			FINISHED BLOCK SIZE: *Single dimensions in the cutting chart indicate the size of the cut square (3" = 3" x 3")*					
			6"	8"	9"	10"	12"	14"
Light	A: 1		2¾"	3¼"	3½"	3¾"	4¼"	4¾"
	B: 8		1⅝"	1⅞"	2"	2⅛"	2⅜"	2⅝"
	C: 4		1¼"	1½"	1⅝"	1¾"	2"	2¼"
	D: 5		T5	T7	T8	T9	T11	T12
Medium	E: 12		1⅝"	1⅞"	2"	2⅛"	2⅜"	2⅝"
Dark	F: 2		3⅛"	3⅞"	4¼"	4⅝"	5⅜"	6⅛"
	G: 4		T5	T7	T8	T9	T11	T12
Try this:			Use a medium instead of a dark for F.					

The Square Deal

8-Unit Grid

Color Illustration: page 23

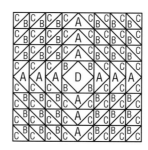

FOR 1 BLOCK:			FINISHED BLOCK SIZE: *Single dimensions in the cutting chart indicate the size of the cut square (3" = 3" x 3")*					
			6"	8"	9"	10"	12"	14"
Light	A: 3		2¾"	3¼"	3½"	3¾"	4¼"	4¾"
	B: 20		1⅝"	1⅞"	2"	2⅛"	2⅜"	2⅝"
Dark	C: 30		1⅝"	1⅞"	2"	2⅛"	2⅜"	2⅝"
	D: 1		T5	T7	T8	T9	T11	T12
Try this:			Use many different darks for C.					

☐ *Light* ▥ *Light 2* ▦ *Medium* ▨ *Medium 2* ■ *Dark*

Square and Star

4-Unit Grid

Color Illustration: page 23

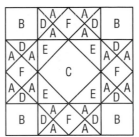

For 1 block:			FINISHED BLOCK SIZE: Single dimensions in the cutting chart indicate the size of the cut square (3" = 3" x 3")					
			4"	6"	8"	9"	10"	12"
Light	A: 4 ⊠→⊠		2¼"	2¾"	3¼"	3½"	3¾"	4¼"
	B: 4 ☐		1½"	2"	2½"	2¾"	3"	3½"
	C: 1 ◇		T7	T11	T14	T15	T16	T19
Dark	D: 2 ⊠→⊠		2¼"	2¾"	3¼"	3½"	3¾"	4¼"
	E: 2 ◻→◸		1⅞"	2⅜"	2⅞"	3⅛"	3⅜"	3⅞"
	F: 4 ◇		T2	T5	T7	T8	T9	T11
Try this:	Use a medium instead of a dark for F.							

Squirrel in a Cage

6-Unit Grid

Color Illustration: page 24

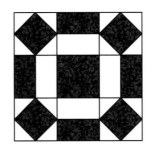
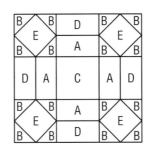
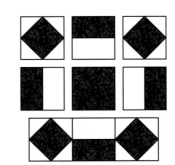

For 1 block:			FINISHED BLOCK SIZE: Single dimensions in the cutting chart indicate the size of the cut square (3" = 3" x 3")					
			4½"	6"	7½"	9"	10½"	12"
Light	A: 4 ☐		1¼" x 2"	1½" x 2½"	1¾" x 3"	2" x 3½"	2¼" x 4"	2½" x 4½"
	B: 8 ◻→◸		1⅝"	1⅞"	2⅛"	2⅜"	2⅝"	2⅞"
Dark	C: 1 ☐		2"	2½"	3"	3½"	4"	4½"
	D: 4 ☐		1¼" x 2"	1½" x 2½"	1¾" x 3"	2" x 3½"	2¼" x 4"	2½" x 4½"
	E: 4 ◇		T5	T7	T9	T11	T12	T14
Try this:	Reverse the lights and darks in every other block.							

109

The Star and Block

4-Unit Grid
Color Illustration: page 24

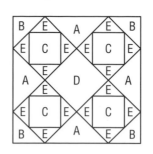

FOR 1 BLOCK:			FINISHED BLOCK SIZE: *Single dimensions in the cutting chart indicate the size of the cut square (3" = 3" x 3")*					
			4"	**6"**	**8"**	**9"**	**10"**	**12"**
Light	A: 1		3¼"	4¼"	5¼"	5¾"	6¼"	7¼"
	B: 2		1⅞"	2⅜"	2⅞"	3⅛"	3⅜"	3⅞"
	C: 4		1½"	2"	2½"	2¾"	3"	3½"
	D: 1		T7	T11	T14	T15	T16	T19
Dark	E: 4		2¼"	2¾"	3¼"	3½"	3¾"	4¼"
Try this:	Use a different dark fabric in each corner of the block.							

Star of Virginia

6-Unit Grid
Color Illustration: page 24

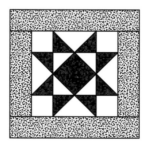
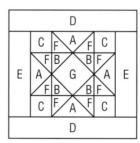

FOR 1 BLOCK:			FINISHED BLOCK SIZE: *Single dimensions in the cutting chart indicate the size of the cut square (3" = 3" x 3")*					
			4½"	**6"**	**7½"**	**9"**	**10½"**	**12"**
Light	A: 1		2¾"	3¼"	3¾"	4¼"	4¾"	5¼"
	B: 2		1⅝"	1⅞"	2⅛"	2⅜"	2⅝"	2⅞"
	C: 4		1¼"	1½"	1¾"	2"	2¼"	2½"
Medium	D: 2		1¼" x 5"	1½" x 6½"	1¾" x 8"	2" x 9½"	2¼" x 11"	2½" x 12½"
	E: 2		1¼" x 3½"	1½" x 4½"	1¾" x 5½"	2" x 6½"	2¼" x 7½"	2½" x 8½"
Dark	F: 4		1⅝"	1⅞"	2⅛"	2⅜"	2⅝"	2⅞"
	G: 1		T5	T7	T9	T11	T12	T14
Try this:	Reverse the mediums and darks in every other block.							

☐ Light   ░ Light 2   ▦ Medium   ▨ Medium 2   ■ Dark

Star X

3-Unit Grid
Color Illustration: page 24

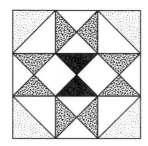

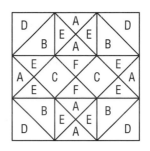

FOR 2 BLOCKS:			**FINISHED BLOCK SIZE:** *Single dimensions in the cutting chart indicate the size of the cut square (3" = 3" x 3")*					
			4½"	**6"**	**7½"**	**9"**	**10½"**	**12"**
Light	A: 3 ▤→▧		2¾"	3¼"	3¾"	4¼"	4¾"	5¼"
	B: 4 ▱→▨		2⅜"	2⅞"	3⅜"	3⅞"	4⅜"	4⅞"
	C: 4 ◇		T5	T7	T9	T11	T12	T14
Light 2	D: 4 ▱→◹		2⅜"	2⅞"	3⅜"	3⅞"	4⅜"	4⅞"
Medium	E: 4 ▤→▧		2¾"	3¼"	3¾"	4¼"	4¾"	5¼"
Dark	F: 1 ▤→▧		2¾"	3¼"	3¾"	4¼"	4¾"	5¼"
Try this:	Use a dark instead of a light 2 for D.							

Storm Signal

6-Unit Grid
Color Illustration: page 24

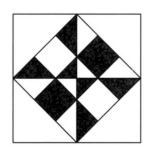

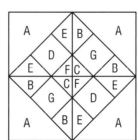

FOR 1 BLOCK:			**FINISHED BLOCK SIZE:** *Single dimensions in the cutting chart indicate the size of the cut square (3" = 3" x 3")*					
			4½"	**6"**	**7½"**	**9"**	**10½"**	**12"**
Light	A: 2 ▱→◹		3⅛"	3⅞"	4⅝"	5⅜"	6⅛"	6⅞"
	B: 1 ▤→▧		2¾"	3¼"	3¾"	4¼"	4¾"	5¼"
	C: 1 ▱→◹		1⅝"	1⅞"	2⅛"	2⅜"	2⅝"	2⅞"
	D: 2 ◇		T5	T7	T9	T11	T12	T14
Dark	E: 1 ▤→▧		2¾"	3¼"	3¾"	4¼"	4¾"	5¼"
	F: 1 ▱→◹		1⅝"	1⅞"	2⅛"	2⅜"	2⅝"	2⅞"
	G: 2 ◇		T5	T7	T9	T11	T12	T14
Try this:	Use a medium instead of a light for A.							

Sunshine

8-Unit Grid

Color Illustration: page 24

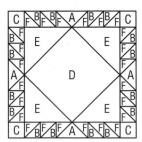

FOR 1 BLOCK:			FINISHED BLOCK SIZE: *Single dimensions in the cutting chart indicate the size of the cut square (3" = 3" x 3")*					
			6"	8"	9"	10"	12"	14"
Light	A: 1		2¾"	3¼"	3½"	3¾"	4¼"	4¾"
	B: 8		1⅝"	1⅞"	2"	2⅛"	2⅜"	2⅝"
	C: 4		1¼"	1½"	1⅝"	1¾"	2"	2¼"
	D: 1		T15	T19	T20	T22	T24	T26
Dark	E: 2		3⅛"	3⅞"	4¼"	4⅝"	5⅜"	6⅛"
	F: 12		1⅝"	1⅞"	2"	2⅛"	2⅜"	2⅝"
Try this:		Use a medium- or large-scale print for D.						

T Square

8-Unit Grid

Color Illustration: page 24

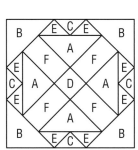

FOR 1 BLOCK:			FINISHED BLOCK SIZE: *Single dimensions in the cutting chart indicate the size of the cut square (3" = 3" x 3")*					
			6"	8"	9"	10"	12"	14"
Light	A: 1		4¼"	5¼"	5¾"	6¼"	7¼"	8¼"
	B: 2		3⅛"	3⅞"	4¼"	4⅝"	5⅜"	6⅛"
	C: 1		2¾"	3¼"	3½"	3¾"	4¼"	4¾"
	D: 1		T5	T7	T8	T9	T11	T12
Dark	E: 2		2¾"	3¼"	3½"	3¾"	4¼"	4¾"
	F: 4		T41	T51	T56	T59	T67	T70
Try this:		Use one light for A and D and a different light for B and C.						

 Light   Light 2   Medium   Medium 2   Dark

Temple Court

8-Unit Grid
Color Illustration: page 24

 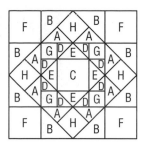 

		FINISHED BLOCK SIZE:					
		Single dimensions in the cutting chart indicate the size of the cut square (3" = 3" x 3")					
FOR 1 BLOCK:		6"	8"	9"	10"	12"	14"
Light	A: 2 ⊠→⊠	2¾"	3¼"	3½"	3¾"	4¼"	4¾"
	B: 4 ◻→◺	2⅜"	2⅞"	3⅛"	3⅜"	3⅞"	4⅜"
	C: 1 ◻	2"	2½"	2¾"	3"	3½"	4"
	D: 4 ◻→◺	1⅝"	1⅞"	2"	2⅛"	2⅜"	2⅝"
Dark	E: 1 ⊠→⊠	2¾"	3¼"	3½"	3¾"	4¼"	4¾"
	F: 4 ◻	2"	2½"	2¾"	3"	3½"	4"
	G: 4 ◻	1¼"	1½"	1⅝"	1¾"	2"	2¼"
	H: 4 ◇	T5	T7	T8	T9	T11	T12
Try this:	Use a medium instead of a light for A.						

Thunder and Lightning

6-Unit Grid
Color Illustration: page 24

 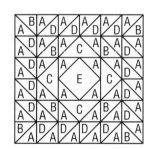 

		FINISHED BLOCK SIZE:					
		Single dimensions in the cutting chart indicate the size of the cut square (3" = 3" x 3")					
FOR 1 BLOCK:		4½"	6"	7½"	9"	10½"	12"
Light	A: 18 ◻→◺	1⅝"	1⅞"	2⅛"	2⅜"	2⅝"	2⅞"
Medium	B: 4 ◻→◺	1⅝"	1⅞"	2⅛"	2⅜"	2⅝"	2⅞"
Dark	C: 1 ⊠→⊠	2¾"	3¼"	3¾"	4¼"	4¾"	5¼"
	D: 8 ◻→◺	1⅝"	1⅞"	2⅛"	2⅜"	2⅝"	2⅞"
	E: 1 ◇	T5	T7	T9	T11	T12	T14
Try this:	Use one dark for C and E and a different dark for D.						

Tinted Chains
8-Unit Grid
Color Illustration: page 24

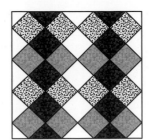
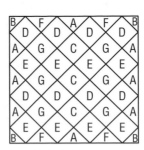
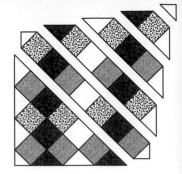

FOR 1 BLOCK:			FINISHED BLOCK SIZE: *Single dimensions in the cutting chart indicate the size of the cut square (3" = 3" x 3")*					
			6"	**8"**	**9"**	**10"**	**12"**	**14"**
Light	A: 2		2¾"	3¼"	3½"	3¾"	4¼"	4¾"
	B: 2		1⅝"	1⅞"	2"	2⅛"	2⅜"	2⅝"
	C: 3		T5	T7	T8	T9	T11	T12
Medium	D: 8		T5	T7	T8	T9	T11	T12
Medium 2	E: 8		T5	T7	T8	T9	T11	T12
Dark	F: 1		2¾"	3¼"	3½"	3¾"	4¼"	4¾"
	G: 6		T5	T7	T8	T9	T11	T12
Try this:	Use many different fabrics for D and E.							

Toad in a Puddle

4-Unit Grid
Color Illustration: page 24

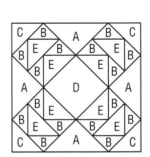

FOR 1 BLOCK:			FINISHED BLOCK SIZE: *Single dimensions in the cutting chart indicate the size of the cut square (3" = 3" x 3")*					
			4"	**6"**	**8"**	**9"**	**10"**	**12"**
Light	A: 1		3¼"	4¼"	5¼"	5¾"	6¼"	7¼"
	B: 4		2¼"	2¾"	3¼"	3½"	3¾"	4¼"
	C: 2		1⅞"	2⅜"	2⅞"	3⅛"	3⅜"	3⅞"
	D: 1		T7	T11	T14	T15	T16	T19
Dark	E: 4		1⅞"	2⅜"	2⅞"	3⅛"	3⅜"	3⅞"
Try this:	Use a medium instead of a light for A and C.							

☐ Light ▨ Light 2 ▩ Medium ▨ Medium 2 ■ Dark

Tombstone Quilt

4-Unit Grid

Color Illustration: page 24

 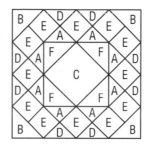 

FOR 1 BLOCK:			FINISHED BLOCK SIZE: *Single dimensions in the cutting chart indicate the size of the cut square (3" = 3" x 3")*					
			4"	**6"**	**8"**	**9"**	**10"**	**12"**
Light	A: 2		2¼"	2¾"	3¼"	3½"	3¾"	4¼"
	B: 2		1⅞"	2⅜"	2⅞"	3⅛"	3⅜"	3⅞"
	C: 1		T7	T11	T14	T15	T16	T19
Medium	D: 2		2¼"	2¾"	3¼"	3½"	3¾"	4¼"
	E: 12		T2	T5	T7	T8	T9	T11
Dark	F: 2		1⅞"	2⅜"	2⅞"	3⅛"	3⅜"	3⅞"
Try this:		Use several different mediums for E.						

Totem

6-Unit Grid

Color Illustration: page 25

 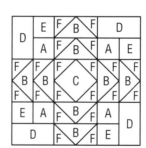 

FOR 1 BLOCK:			FINISHED BLOCK SIZE: *Single dimensions in the cutting chart indicate the size of the cut square (3" = 3" x 3")*					
			4½"	**6"**	**7½"**	**9"**	**10½"**	**12"**
Light	A: 4		1¼"	1½"	1¾"	2"	2¼"	2½"
Light 2	B: 2		2¾"	3¼"	3¾"	4¼"	4¾"	5¼"
	C: 1		T5	T7	T9	T11	T12	T14
Medium	D: 4		1¼" x 2"	1½" x 2½"	1¾" x 3"	2" x 3½"	2¼" x 4"	2½" x 4½"
	E: 4		1¼"	1½"	1¾"	2"	2¼"	2½"
Dark	F: 10		1⅝"	1⅞"	2⅛"	2⅜"	2⅝"	2⅞"
Try this:		Reverse the light and the mediums in every other block.						

Twelve Triangles

4-Unit Grid

Color Illustration: page 25

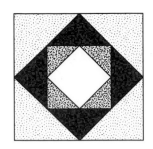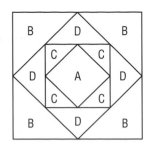

		FINISHED BLOCK SIZE: *Single dimensions in the cutting chart indicate the size of the cut square (3" = 3" x 3")*					
FOR 1 BLOCK:		**4"**	**6"**	**8"**	**9"**	**10"**	**12"**
Light	A: 1 ◇	T7	T11	T14	T15	T16	T19
Light 2	B: 2 ◻→◺	2⅞"	3⅞"	4⅞"	5⅜"	5⅞"	6⅞"
Medium	C: 2 ◻→◺	1⅞"	2⅜"	2⅞"	3⅛"	3⅜"	3⅞"
Dark	D: 1 ⊠→⧅	3¼"	4¼"	5¼"	5¾"	6¼"	7¼"
Try this:	Use a different combination of fabrics in every block.						

Union Square

3-Unit Grid

Color Illustration: page 25

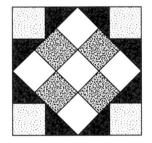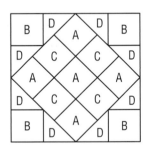

		FINISHED BLOCK SIZE: *Single dimensions in the cutting chart indicate the size of the cut square (3" = 3" x 3")*					
FOR 1 BLOCK:		**4½"**	**6"**	**7½"**	**9"**	**10½"**	**12"**
Light	A: 5 ◇	T5	T7	T9	T11	T12	T14
Light 2	B: 4 ◻	1⅝"	2"	2⅜"	2¾"	3⅛"	3½"
Medium	C: 4 ◇	T5	T7	T9	T11	T12	T14
Dark	D: 4 ◻→◺	2"	2⅜"	2¾"	3⅛"	3½"	3⅞"
Try this:	Reverse the mediums and darks in every other block.						

◻ Light	▥ Light 2	▦ Medium	▨ Medium 2	■ Dark

Variable Star

4-Unit Grid

Color Illustration: page 25

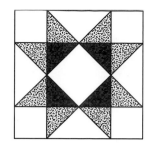 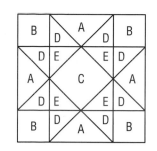

FOR 1 BLOCK:			FINISHED BLOCK SIZE: *Single dimensions in the cutting chart indicate the size of the cut square (3" = 3" x 3")*					
			4"	6"	8"	9"	10"	12"
Light	A: 1		3¼"	4¼"	5¼"	5¾"	6¼"	7¼"
	B: 4		1½"	2"	2½"	2¾"	3"	3½"
	C: 1		T7	T11	T14	T15	T16	T19
Medium	D: 4		1⅞"	2⅜"	2⅞"	3⅛"	3⅜"	3⅞"
Dark	E: 2		1⅞"	2⅜"	2⅞"	3⅛"	3⅜"	3⅞"
Try this:		Use one light for A and B and a different light for C.						

Virginia Reel

8-Unit Grid

Color Illustration: page 25

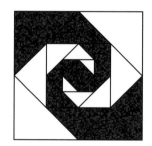 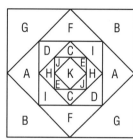 

FOR 2 BLOCKS:			FINISHED BLOCK SIZE: *Single dimensions in the cutting chart indicate the size of the cut square (3" = 3" x 3")*					
			6"	8"	9"	10"	12"	14"
Light	A: 1		4¼"	5¼"	5¾"	6¼"	7¼"	8¼"
	B: 2		3⅞"	4⅞"	5⅜"	5⅞"	6⅞"	7⅞"
	C: 1		2¾"	3¼"	3½"	3¾"	4¼"	4¾"
	D: 2		2⅜"	2⅞"	3⅛"	3⅜"	3⅞"	4⅜"
	E: 2		1⅝"	1⅞"	2"	2⅛"	2⅜"	2⅝"
Dark	F: 1		4¼"	5¼"	5¾"	6¼"	7¼"	8¼"
	G: 2		3⅞"	4⅞"	5⅜"	5⅞"	6⅞"	7⅞"
	H: 1		2¾"	3¼"	3½"	3¾"	4¼"	4¾"
	I: 2		2⅜"	2⅞"	3⅛"	3⅜"	3⅞"	4⅜"
	J: 2		1⅝"	1⅞"	2"	2⅛"	2⅜"	2⅝"
	K: 2		T5	T7	T8	T9	T11	T12
Try this:		Use a medium and a dark instead of a light and a dark.						

Washington Pavement

8-Unit Grid

Color Illustration: page 25

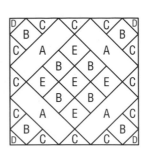

FOR 1 BLOCK:		FINISHED BLOCK SIZE: *Single dimensions in the cutting chart indicate the size of the cut square (3" = 3" x 3")*					
		6"	**8"**	**9"**	**10"**	**12"**	**14"**
Light	A: 4 ◇	T42	T52	T57	T60	T68	T71
	B: 8 ◇	T5	T7	T8	T9	T11	T12
Dark	C: 3 ⊠→⊠	2¾"	3¼"	3½"	3¾"	4¼"	4¾"
	D: 2 ◻→◺	1⅝"	1⅞"	2"	2⅛"	2⅜"	2⅝"
	E: 5 ◇	T5	T7	T8	T9	T11	T12
Try this:		Use a different combination of lights and darks in every block.					

The Wedding Ring

4-Unit Grid

Color Illustration: page 25

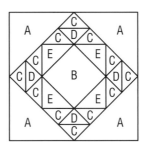

FOR 1 BLOCK:		FINISHED BLOCK SIZE: *Single dimensions in the cutting chart indicate the size of the cut square (3" = 3" x 3")*					
		4"	**6"**	**8"**	**9"**	**10"**	**12"**
Light	A: 2 ◻→◺	2⅞"	3⅞"	4⅞"	5⅜"	5⅞"	6⅞"
	B: 1 ◇	T7	T11	T14	T15	T16	T19
Medium	C: 3 ⊠→⊠	2¼"	2¾"	3¼"	3½"	3¾"	4¼"
Dark	D: 1 ⊠→⊠	2¼"	2¾"	3¼"	3½"	3¾"	4¼"
	E: 2 ◻→◺	1⅞"	2⅜"	2⅞"	3⅛"	3⅜"	3⅞"
Try this:		Use one light for A and a different light for B.					

☐ *Light* ▦ *Light 2* ▨ *Medium* ▩ *Medium 2* ■ *Dark*

Whirling Squares

4-Unit Grid

Color Illustration: page 25

 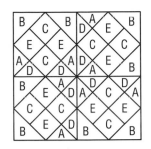 

FOR 1 BLOCK:			**FINISHED BLOCK SIZE:** *Single dimensions in the cutting chart indicate the size of the cut square (3" = 3" x 3")*					
			4"	**6"**	**8"**	**9"**	**10"**	**12"**
Light	A: 2 ⊠→⊠		2¼"	2¾"	3¼"	3½"	3¾"	4¼"
	B: 4 ◻→◺		1⅞"	2⅜"	2⅞"	3⅛"	3⅜"	3⅞"
	C: 8 ◇		T2	T5	T7	T8	T9	T11
Dark	D: 2 ⊠→⊠		2¼"	2¾"	3¼"	3½"	3¾"	4¼"
	E: 8 ◇		T2	T5	T7	T8	T9	T11
Try this:	Use a medium instead of a light for C.							

Whirlwind

10-Unit Grid

Color Illustration: page 26

 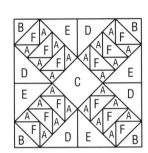 

FOR 1 BLOCK:			**FINISHED BLOCK SIZE:** *Single dimensions in the cutting chart indicate the size of the cut square (3" = 3" x 3")*					
			6¼"	**7½"**	**8¾"**	**10"**	**12½"**	**13¾"**
Light	A: 6 ⊠→⊠		2½"	2¾"	3"	3¼"	3¾"	4"
	B: 2 ◻→◺		2⅛"	2⅜"	2⅝"	2⅞"	3⅜"	3⅝"
	C: 1 ◇		T9	T11	T12	T14	T16	T18
Medium	D: 2 ◻→◺		2¾"	3⅛"	3½"	3⅞"	4⅝"	5"
Medium 2	E: 2 ◻→◺		2¾"	3⅛"	3½"	3⅞"	4⅝"	5"
Dark	F: 6 ◻→◺		2⅛"	2⅜"	2⅝"	2⅞"	3⅜"	3⅝"
Try this:	Use several different lights for A.							

Wild Goose

4-Unit Grid

Color Illustration: page 26

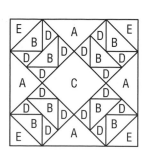

FOR 1 BLOCK:		**FINISHED BLOCK SIZE:** *Single dimensions in the cutting chart indicate the size of the cut square (3" = 3" x 3")*					
		4"	**6"**	**8"**	**9"**	**10"**	**12"**
Light	A: 1 ⊠→⊠	3¼"	4¼"	5¼"	5¾"	6¼"	7¼"
	B: 4 □→◩	1⅞"	2⅜"	2⅞"	3⅛"	3⅜"	3⅞"
	C: 1 ◇	T7	T11	T14	T15	T16	T19
Dark	D: 4 ⊠→⊠	2¼"	2¾"	3¼"	3½"	3¾"	4¼"
	E: 2 □→◩	1⅞"	2⅜"	2⅞"	3⅛"	3⅜"	3⅞"
Try this:	Reverse the lights and darks.						

Wild Goose Chase II

6-Unit Grid

Color Illustration: page 26

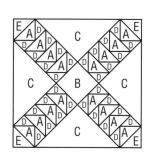

FOR 1 BLOCK:		**FINISHED BLOCK SIZE:** *Single dimensions in the cutting chart indicate the size of the cut square (3" = 3" x 3")*					
		4½"	**6"**	**7½"**	**9"**	**10½"**	**12"**
Light	A: 8 □→◪	1⅝"	1⅞"	2⅛"	2⅜"	2⅝"	2⅞"
	B: 1 ◇	T5	T7	T9	T11	T12	T14
Medium	C: 1 ⊠→⊠	4¼"	5¼"	6¼"	7¼"	8¼"	9¼"
Dark	D: 8 ⊠→⊠	2"	2¼"	2½"	2¾"	3"	3¼"
	E: 2 □→◩	1⅝"	1⅞"	2⅛"	2⅜"	2⅝"	2⅞"
Try this:	Reverse the lights and the medium.						

122

□ Light ⬚ Light 2 ▨ Medium ▨ Medium 2 ■ Dark

Wild Goose Chase III

6-Unit Grid

Color Illustration: page 26

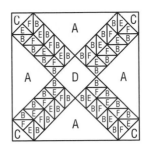

FOR 1 BLOCK:			FINISHED BLOCK SIZE: *Single dimensions in the cutting chart indicate the size of the cut square (3" = 3" x 3")*					
			4½"	**6"**	**7½"**	**9"**	**10½"**	**12"**
Light	A: 1		4¼"	5¼"	6¼"	7¼"	8¼"	9¼"
	B: 8		2"	2¼"	2½"	2¾"	3"	3¼"
	C: 2		1⅝"	1⅞"	2⅛"	2⅜"	2⅝"	2⅞"
	D: 1		T5	T7	T9	T11	T12	T14
Medium	E: 4		2"	2¼"	2½"	2¾"	3"	3¼"
Dark	F: 4		2"	2¼"	2½"	2¾"	3"	3¼"
Try this:		Use many different fabrics for E and F.						

Willow Haven

4-Unit Grid

Color Illustration: page 26

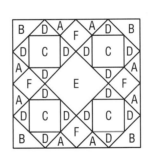

FOR 1 BLOCK:			FINISHED BLOCK SIZE: *Single dimensions in the cutting chart indicate the size of the cut square (3" = 3" x 3")*					
			4"	**6"**	**8"**	**9"**	**10"**	**12"**
Light	A: 2		2¼"	2¾"	3¼"	3½"	3¾"	4¼"
	B: 2		1⅞"	2⅜"	2⅞"	3⅛"	3⅜"	3⅞"
	C: 4		1½"	2"	2½"	2¾"	3"	3½"
Medium	D: 4		2¼"	2¾"	3¼"	3½"	3¾"	4¼"
Dark	E: 1		T7	T11	T14	T15	T16	T19
	F: 4		T2	T5	T7	T8	T9	T11
Try this:		Use one dark for E and a different dark for F.						

Windblown Square

4-Unit Grid

Color Illustration: page 26

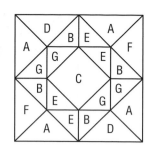

FOR 2 BLOCKS:			FINISHED BLOCK SIZE: *Single dimensions in the cutting chart indicate the size of the cut square (3" = 3" x 3")*					
			4"	**6"**	**8"**	**9"**	**10"**	**12"**
Light	A: 2	⊠→⊠	3¼"	4¼"	5¼"	5¾"	6¼"	7¼"
	B: 4	◻→◸	1⅞"	2⅜"	2⅞"	3⅛"	3⅜"	3⅞"
	C: 2	◇	T7	T11	T14	T15	T16	T19
Medium	D: 1	⊠→⊠	3¼"	4¼"	5¼"	5¾"	6¼"	7¼"
	E: 4	◻→◸	1⅞"	2⅜"	2⅞"	3⅛"	3⅜"	3⅞"
Dark	F: 1	⊠→⊠	3¼"	4¼"	5¼"	5¾"	6¼"	7¼"
	G: 4	◻→◸	1⅞"	2⅜"	2⅞"	3⅛"	3⅜"	3⅞"
Try this:			Use one light for A and C and a different light for B.					

Windows and Doors

10-Unit Grid

Color Illustration: page 26

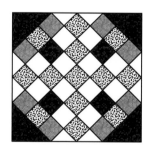
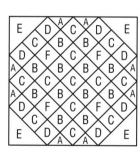

FOR 1 BLOCK:			FINISHED BLOCK SIZE: *Single dimensions in the cutting chart indicate the size of the cut square (3" = 3" x 3")*					
			6¼"	**7½"**	**8¾"**	**10"**	**12½"**	**13¾"**
Light	A: 2	⊠→⊠	2½"	2¾"	3"	3¼"	3¾"	4"
	B: 12	◇	T4	T5	T6	T7	T9	T10
Medium	C: 13	◇	T4	T5	T6	T7	T9	T10
Medium 2	D: 8	◇	T4	T5	T6	T7	T9	T10
Dark	E: 2	◻→◸	2¾"	3⅛"	3½"	3⅞"	4⅝"	5"
	F: 4	◇	T4	T5	T6	T7	T9	T10
Try this:			Use many different mediums for C and D.					

◻ Light   ⬚ Light 2   ▨ Medium   ▣ Medium 2   ■ Dark

Woodland Path

10-Unit Grid
Color Illustration: page 26

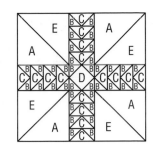

			FINISHED BLOCK SIZE: *Single dimensions in the cutting chart indicate the size of the cut square (3" = 3" x 3")*					
FOR 1 BLOCK:			**6¼"**	**7½"**	**8¾"**	**10"**	**12½"**	**13¾"**
Light	A: 2	◻→◻	3⅜"	3⅞"	4⅜"	4⅞"	5⅞"	6⅜"
	B: 18	◻→◻	1½"	1⅝"	1¾"	1⅞"	2⅛"	2¼"
Medium	C: 4	⊠→⊠	2½"	2¾"	3"	3¼"	3¾"	4"
	D: 1	◇	T4	T5	T6	T7	T9	T10
Dark	E: 2	◻→◻	3⅜"	3⅞"	4⅜"	4⅞"	5⅞"	6⅜"
Try this:		Use one light for A and a different light for B.						

The X

10-Unit Grid
Color Illustration: page 26

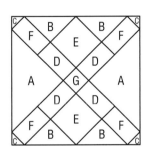

			FINISHED BLOCK SIZE: *Single dimensions in the cutting chart indicate the size of the cut square (3" = 3" x 3")*					
FOR 2 BLOCKS:			**6¼"**	**7½"**	**8¾"**	**10"**	**12½"**	**13¾"**
Light	A: 1	⊠→⊠	6¼"	7¼"	8¼"	9¼"	11¼"	12¼"
	B: 2	⊠→⊠	3¾"	4¼"	4¾"	5¼"	6¼"	6¾"
	C: 4	◻→◻	1½"	1⅝"	1¾"	1⅞"	2⅛"	2¼"
	D: 8	◇	T36	T41	T46	T51	T59	T63
Dark	E: 4	◇	T9	T11	T12	T14	T16	T18
	F: 8	◇	T36	T41	T46	T51	T59	T63
	G: 2	◇	T4	T5	T6	T7	T9	T10
Try this:		Use a medium instead of a light for D.						

Yellow Clover

10-Unit Grid
Color Illustration: page 26

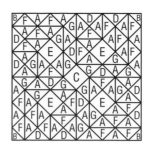

FOR 2 BLOCKS:		**FINISHED BLOCK SIZE:** *Single dimensions in the cutting chart indicate the size of the cut square (3" = 3" x 3")*					
		6¼"	**7½"**	**8¾"**	**10"**	**12½"**	**13¾"**
Light	A: 20 ⊠→⊠	2½"	2¾"	3"	3¼"	3¾"	4"
	B: 4 ◺→◺	1½"	1⅝"	1¾"	1⅞"	2⅛"	2¼"
	C: 2 ◇	T4	T5	T6	T7	T9	T10
Light 2	D: 6 ⊠→⊠	2½"	2¾"	3"	3¼"	3¾"	4"
	E: 8 ◇	T4	T5	T6	T7	T9	T10
Medium	F: 11 ⊠→⊠	2½"	2¾"	3"	3¼"	3¾"	4"
Dark	G: 7 ⊠→⊠	2½"	2¾"	3"	3¼"	3¾"	4"
Try this:	Use a different medium in every block.						

Zenobia's Puzzle

8-Unit Grid
Color Illustration: page 26

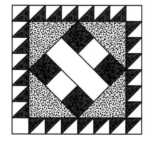
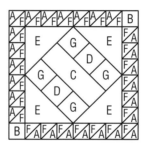

FOR 1 BLOCK:		**FINISHED BLOCK SIZE:** *Single dimensions in the cutting chart indicate the size of the cut square (3" = 3" x 3")*					
		6"	**8"**	**9"**	**10"**	**12"**	**14"**
Light	A: 13 ◺→◺	1⅝"	1⅞"	2"	2⅛"	2⅜"	2⅝"
	B: 2 ☐	1¼"	1½"	1⅝"	1¾"	2"	2¼"
	C: 1 ◇	T42	T52	T57	T60	T68	T71
	D: 2 ◇	T5	T7	T8	T9	T11	T12
Medium	E: 2 ◺→◺	3⅛"	3⅞"	4¼"	4⅝"	5⅜"	6⅛"
Dark	F: 13 ◺→◺	1⅝"	1⅞"	2"	2⅛"	2⅜"	2⅝"
	G: 4 ◇	T5	T7	T8	T9	T11	T12
Try this:	Reverse the lights and darks in every other block.						

☐ Light　▦ Light 2　▩ Medium　▨ Medium 2　■ Dark

Assembling Your Quilt

Squaring Up Blocks

Some quiltmakers find it necessary to trim or square up their blocks before they assemble them into a quilt top. If you trim, be sure to leave ¼"-wide seam allowances beyond any points or other important block details that fall at the outside edges of the block.

Distorted blocks often can be squared up with a little judicious pressing. Cut a piece of plastic-coated freezer paper to the proper size (finished block size plus seam allowance) and iron the freezer paper to your ironing board cover, coated side down. Align block edges with the edges of the freezer-paper guide and pin. Gently steam press. Allow the block to cool before removing pins.

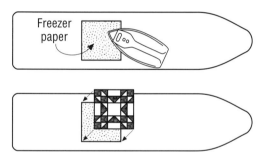

Straight Sets

In straight sets, blocks are laid out in rows that are parallel to the edges of the quilt. Constructing a straight-set quilt is simple. When you set blocks side by side without sashing, stitch them together in rows, then join the rows to complete the patterned section of the quilt. If you are using alternate blocks, cut or piece them to the same size as the primary blocks (including seam allowance), then lay out the primary and alternate blocks in checkerboard fashion, stitch them into rows, then join the rows.

When setting blocks together with plain sashing, cut the vertical sashing pieces the same length as the blocks (including seam allowance) and the desired finished width, plus seam allowance. Join the sashing pieces and the blocks to form rows, starting and ending each row with a block. Then join the rows with long strips of the sashing fabric, cut to the same width as the shorter sashing pieces. Make sure the corners of the blocks are aligned when you stitch the rows together. Add sashing strips to the sides of the quilt top last.

If your sashing includes corner squares of a color or fabric different from the rest of the sashing (sashing squares), cut the vertical sashing pieces and join them to the blocks to form rows, starting and ending each row with a sashing piece. Cut the horizontal sashing pieces the same size as the vertical pieces. Cut sashing squares to the same dimensions as the width of the sashing pieces and join them to the horizontal sashing pieces to make sashing strips, starting and ending each row with a sashing square. Join the rows of blocks with these pieced sashing strips.

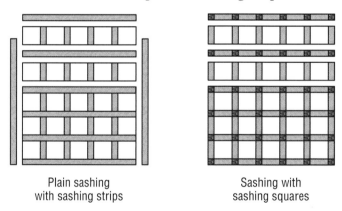

Plain sashing
with sashing strips

Sashing with
sashing squares

On-Point Sets

Quilts that are set on point are constructed in diagonal rows, with pieced half blocks and quarter blocks or plain setting triangles added to complete the sides and corners of the quilt. If you haven't already done so, sketch your quilt on a photocopy of one of the quilt-plan work sheets (pages 131–132) so you can see how the rows go together and how many setting pieces you need.

Plain setting triangles can be quick-cut from squares. You will always need four corner triangles. To maintain straight grain on the outside edges of the quilt, these should be half-square tri-angles. Two squares cut to the proper dimensions, then cut once diagonally, will yield the four half-square triangles needed for the corners.

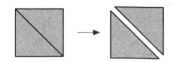

Half-square triangles
for corners

Check your quilt sketch to see how many side triangles you need. To maintain straight grain on the outside edges of the quilt, use quarter-square triangles. A square cut to the proper dimensions and cut twice diagonally will yield four quarter-square triangles. Divide the total number of triangles needed by four, round up to the next whole number, then cut and divide that many squares. In some cases, you will have extra triangles to set aside for another project.

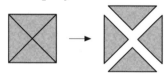

Quarter-square triangles
for sides

How do you determine the proper cutting dimensions for these squares? The calculations are based on the finished size of the blocks, and they vary, depending on whether the blocks are set side by side or are separated by sashing.

For on-point sets where the blocks are set by side with no sashing, determine the proper dimensions to cut the squares as follows:

Corners: Divide the finished block size by 1.414. Add .875 (for seams). Round the result up to the nearest ⅛" (decimal-to-inch conversions appear on page 0). Cut two squares to that size; cut the squares once diagonally.

Sides: Multiply the finished block size by 1.414. Add 1.25 (for seams). Round the result up to the nearest ⅛". Cut squares to that size; cut the squares twice diagonally. Each square yields four triangles.

For on-point sets where the blocks are separated by sashing, determine the proper dimensions to cut the squares as follows:

Corners: Multiply the finished width of the sashing by 2. Add the finished block size. Divide the result by 1.414, then add .875 (for seams), and round up to the nearest ⅛" (decimal-to-inch conversions appear on page 0). Cut two squares to that size; cut the squares once diagonally.

Sides: Add the finished width of the sash to the finished size of the block. Multiply the result by 1.414, add 1.25 (for seams), and round up to the nearest ⅛". Cut squares to that size; cut the squares twice diagonally. Each square yields four triangles.

On-Point Assembly

As noted in the previous section, quilts laid out with the blocks set on point are constructed in diagonal rows. To avoid confusion, lay out all the blocks and setting pieces in the proper configuration before you start sewing. In an on-point set where blocks are set side by side without sashing, simply pick up and sew one row at a time, then join the rows. Trim and square up the outside edges after the rows are sewn, if needed.

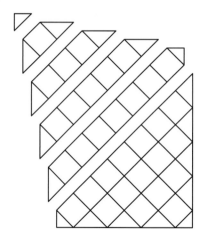

The assembly order for on-point sets that include sashing is a little more complex. You can see from the drawing below that the side setting triangles span a block plus one sashing strip, and the corner triangles span a block plus two sashing pieces. Lay out your blocks, sashing pieces, and setting triangles before sewing so you can see exactly what pieces constitute each row—or make a photocopy of your work sheet and slice it into diagonal rows. Once you have joined the pieces into rows, start joining the rows from the bottom right corner and work toward the center. When you reach the center, set that piece aside and go to the top left corner, again working toward the center. Add the top right and bottom left corner triangles last, after the two main sections have been joined.

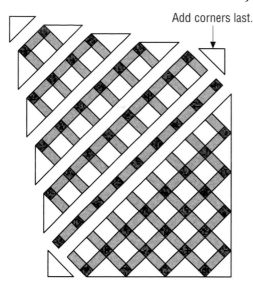

Add corners last.

Assembly diagram for on-point set with sashing

Borders

Most quilters frame the patterned sections of their quilts with plain or pieced border strips. Borders with straight-cut corners are suitable for most quilts, but you may wish to add borders with mitered corners or with corner squares.

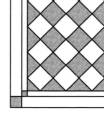

Straight-cut corners   Corner squares   Mitered corners

Because extra yardage is required to cut borders on the lengthwise grain, plain border strips commonly are cut along the crosswise grain and joined end to end when extra length is needed. These seams should be pressed open for minimum visibility. Prepare border strips a few inches longer than you think you'll need; trim them to the proper length once you know the actual dimensions of the patterned section of the quilt. Determine the proper length by measuring across the patterned section at the center, not at the out-

side edges! The outside edges often measure longer than the quilt center due to stretching during construction; if you use these measurements, you are likely to end up with rippled borders and an oddly shaped quilt.

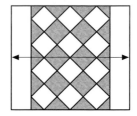
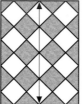

Measure length at center.   Measure width at center after adding side borders.

BORDERS WITH STRAIGHT-CUT CORNERS

To make a border with straight-cut corners, measure the length of the patterned section of the quilt at the center, from raw edge to raw edge. Cut two border strips to that measurement and join them to the sides of the quilt with a ¼"-wide seam, matching the ends and centers and easing the edges to fit. Then, measure the width of the quilt at the center from edge to edge, including the border pieces that you just added. Cut two border strips to that measurement and join them to the top and bottom of the quilt, matching ends and centers and easing as necessary.

BORDERS WITH CORNER SQUARES

To make a border with corner squares, measure the length and width of the patterned section of the quilt at the center, from raw edge to raw edge. Cut two border strips to the lengthwise measurement and join to the sides of the quilt with a ¼"-wide seam, matching the ends and centers and easing the edges to fit. Then cut two border strips to the original crosswise measurement, join corner squares to the ends of the strips, and stitch these units to the top and bottom of the quilt, matching ends, seams, and centers, and easing as necessary.

BORDERS WITH MITERED CORNERS

To make mitered corners, first estimate the finished outside dimensions of your quilt including borders. Cut border strips to this length plus at least ½" for seam allowances; it's safer to add 2" to 3" to give yourself some leeway. If your quilt is to have multiple borders, sew the individual strips together and treat the resulting unit as a single piece for mitering.

Mark the centers of the quilt edges and the centers of the border strips. Stitch the borders to the quilt with a ¼"-wide seam, matching the centers. The border strip should extend the same distance at each end of the quilt. Start and stop your stitching ¼" from the corners of the quilt. Press the seams toward the borders.

Lay the first corner to be mitered on the ironing board, pinning as necessary to keep the quilt from pulling and the corner from slipping. Fold one of the border units under at a 45-degree angle. Work with the fold until any seams or stripes meet properly; pin at the fold, then check to see that the outside corner is square and that there is no extra fullness at the edges. When everything is straight and square, press the fold.

Starting at the outside edge of the quilt, center a piece of 1"-wide masking tape over the mitered fold. Remove pins as you apply the tape.

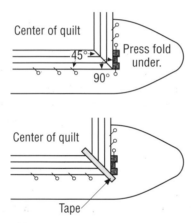

Unpin the quilt from the ironing board and turn it over. Draw a light pencil line on the crease created when you pressed the fold. Fold the center section of the quilt diagonally from the corner, right sides together, and align the long edges of the border strips. Stitch on the pencil line, then remove the tape. Trim the excess fabric and press the seam open. Repeat these steps for the remaining three corners.

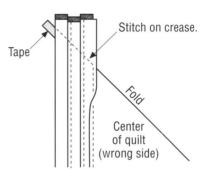

Finishing Your Quilt

As promised, I have taken you from blocks through borders, from the germ of an idea to a completed quilt top. If you need help with marking, layering, quilting, and binding your creation, there are many excellent references that describe the basic techniques. I recommend the "Finishing Your Quilt" section of *101 Fabulous Rotary Cut Quilts* by Judy Hopkins and Nancy J. Martin. Other good references include: *Loving Stitches: A Guide to Fine Hand Quilting* by Jeana Kimball, *Happy Endings—Finishing the Edges of Your Quilt* by Mimi Dietrich, and *The Quilters' Companion* (all That Patchwork Place publications).

Work Sheets for Straight Sets

131

Work Sheets for On-Point Sets

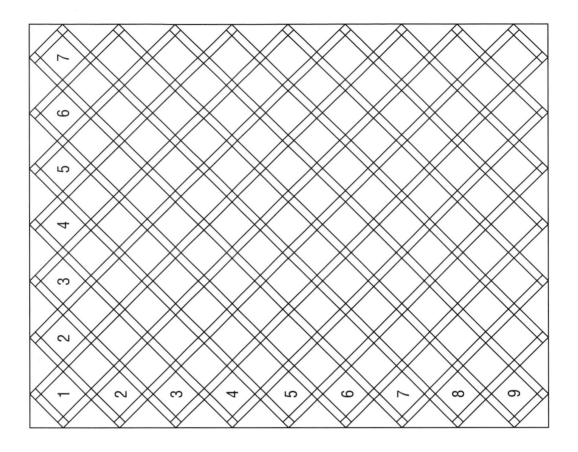

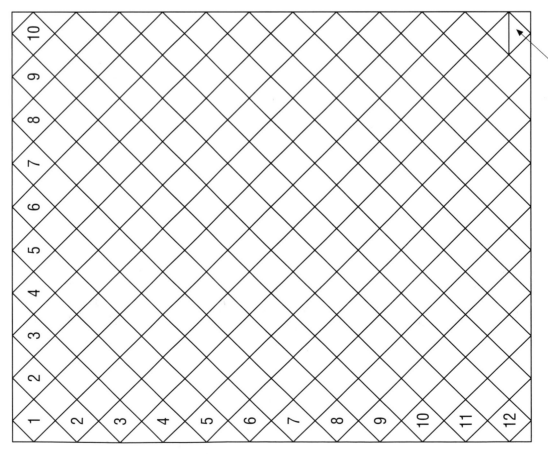

To find finished diagonal measurement of block,
multiply finished block size by 1.414.

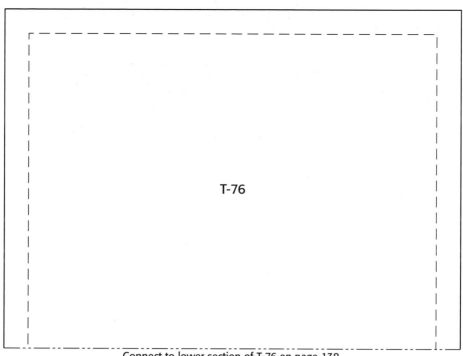

T-76

Connect to lower section of T-76 on page 138.

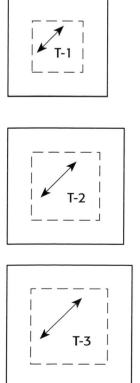

T-1

T-2

T-3

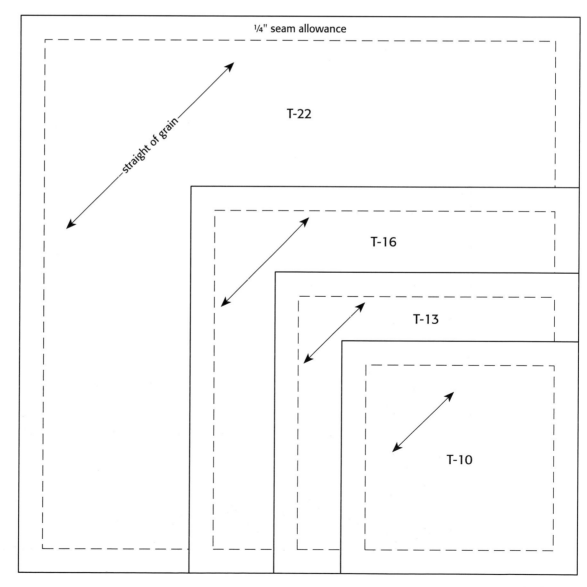

¼" seam allowance

T-22

straight of grain

T-16

T-13

T-10

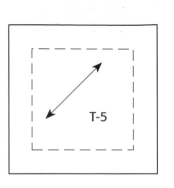

T-5

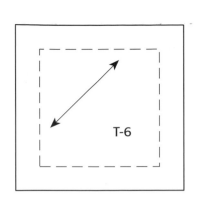

T-6

straight of grain

T-7

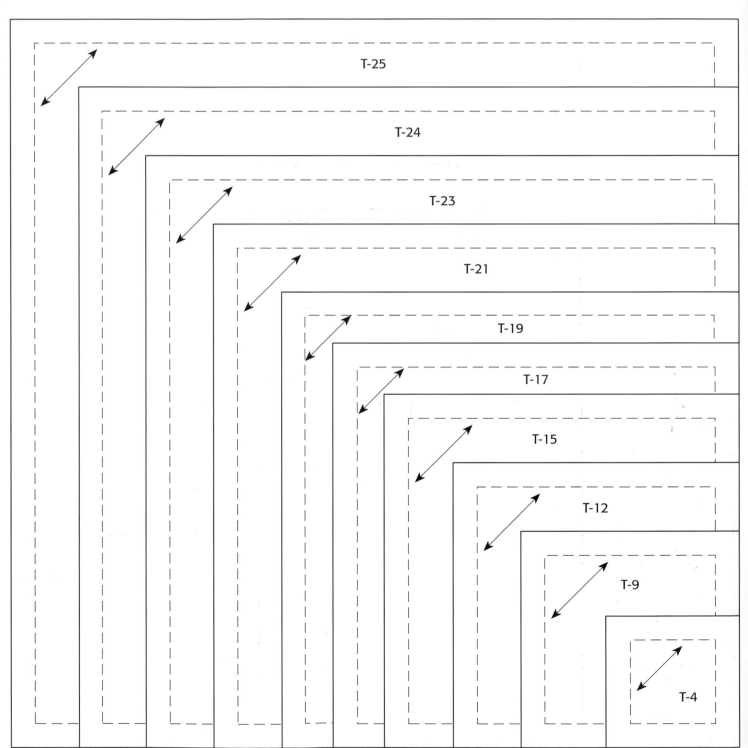

T-25

T-24

T-23

T-21

T-19

T-17

T-15

T-12

T-9

T-4

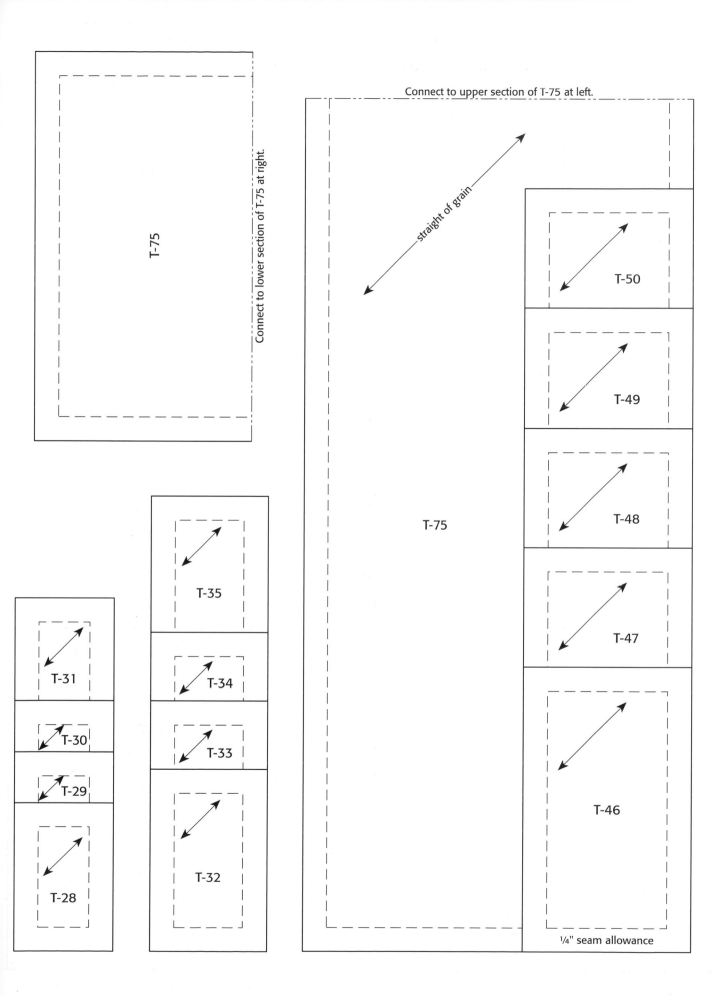

T-75

Connect to lower section of T-75 at right.

Connect to upper section of T-75 at left.

straight of grain

T-75

T-50

T-49

T-48

T-47

T-46

¼" seam allowance

T-35

T-34

T-33

T-32

T-31

T-30

T-29

T-28

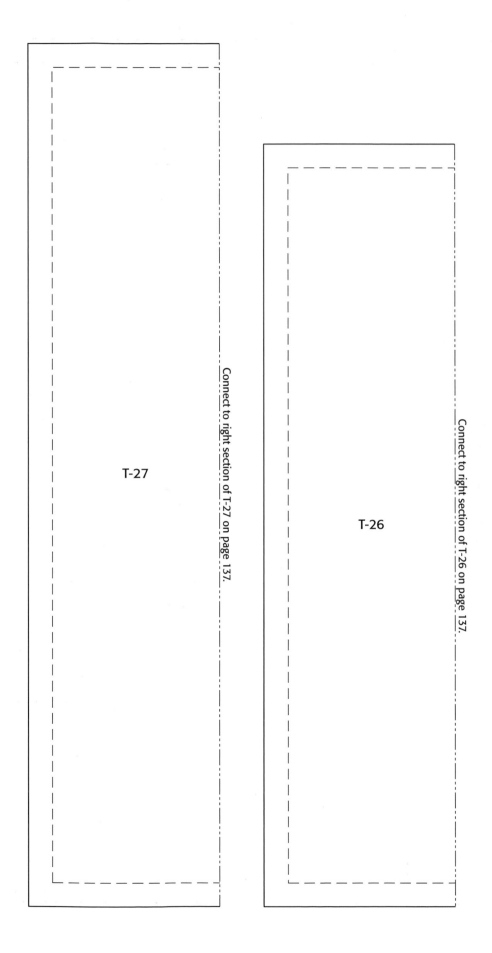

T-27

T-26

Connect to right section of T-27 on page 137.

Connect to right section of T-26 on page 137.

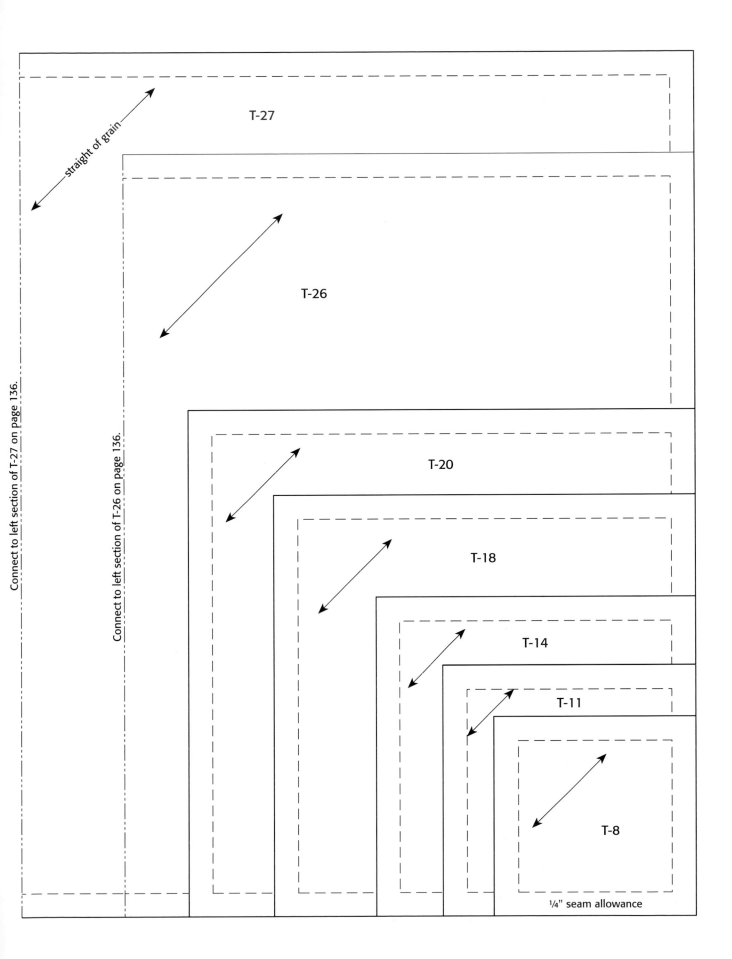

Connect to left section of T-27 on page 136.

Connect to left section of T-26 on page 136.

straight of grain

T-27

T-26

T-20

T-18

T-14

T-11

T-8

¼" seam allowance

137

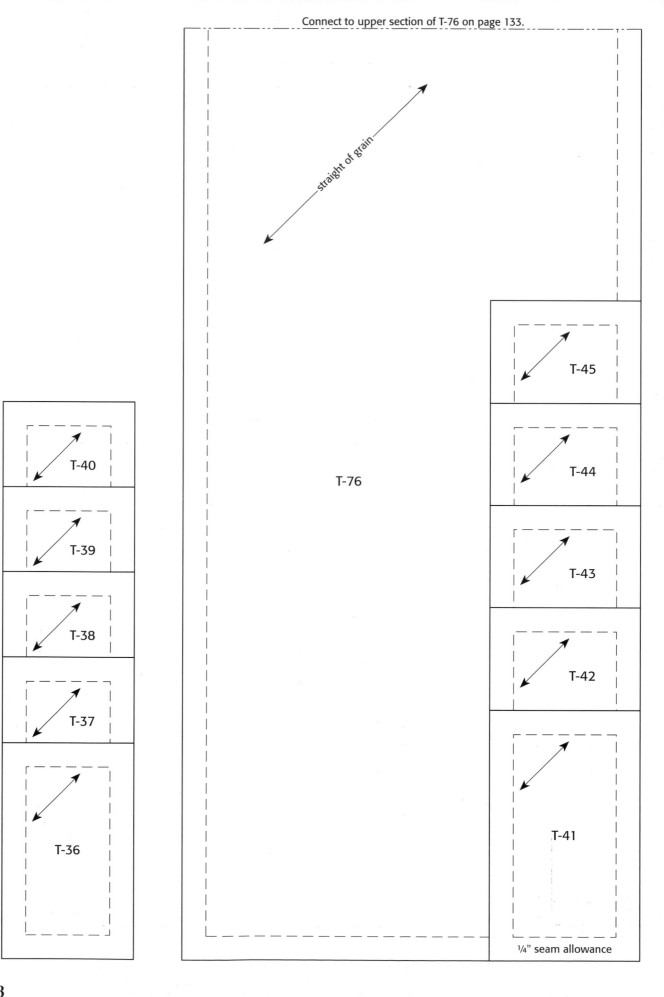

Connect to upper section of T-76 on page 133.

straight of grain

T-76

T-45

T-44

T-43

T-42

T-41

¼" seam allowance

T-40

T-39

T-38

T-37

T-36

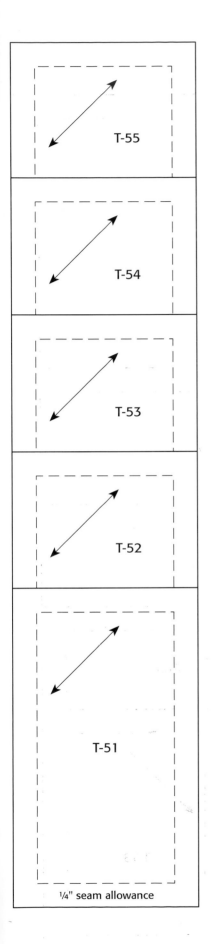

T-55

T-54

T-53

T-52

T-51

¼" seam allowance

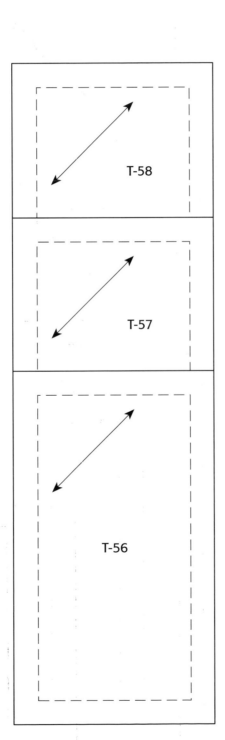

T-58

T-57

T-56

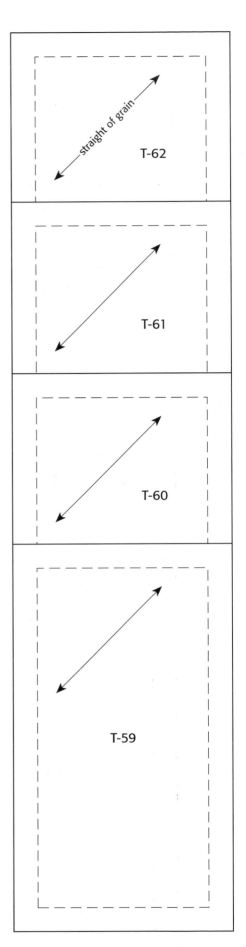

straight of grain

T-62

T-61

T-60

T-59

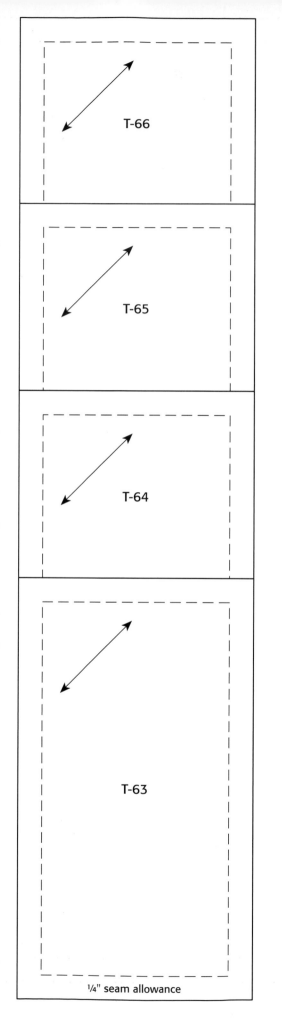

T-66

T-65

T-64

T-63

¼" seam allowance

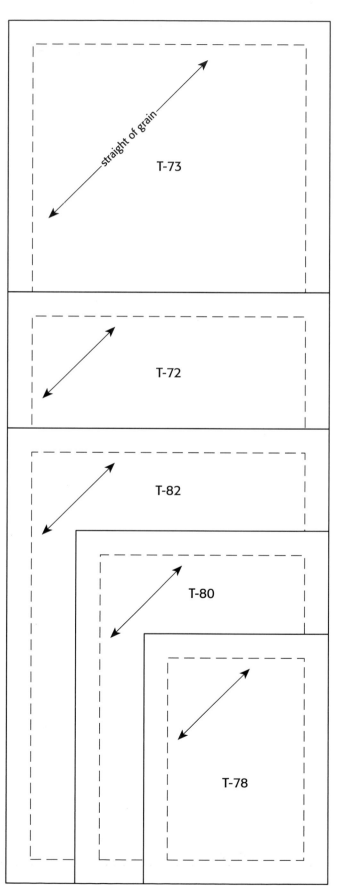

straight of grain

T-73

T-72

T-82

T-80

T-78

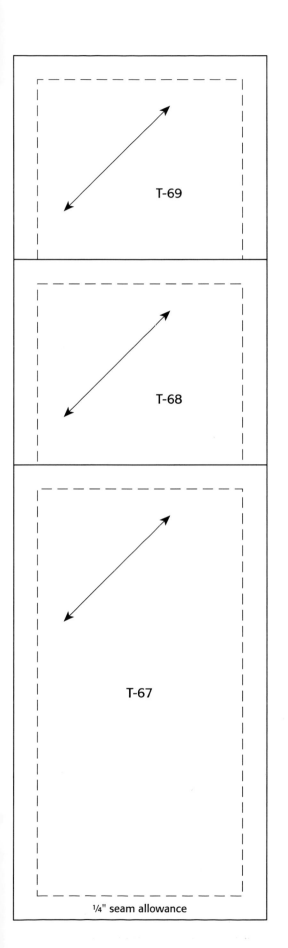

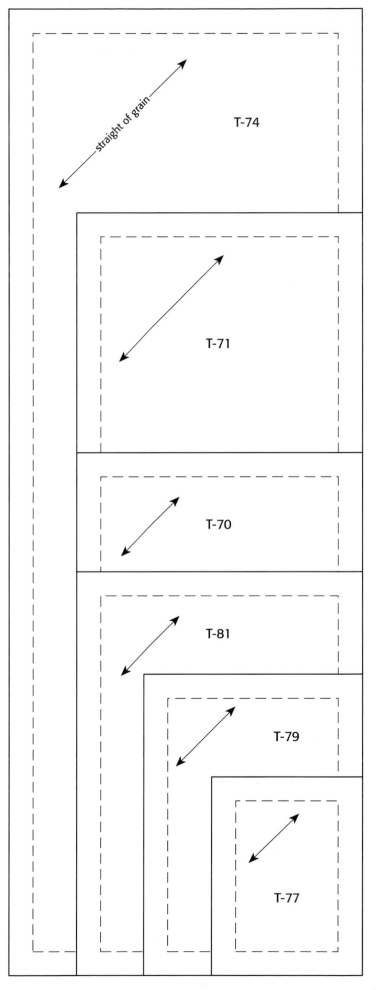

Bibliography

Beyer, Jinny. *The Quilters Album of Blocks and Borders*. McLean, Va.: EPM Publications, 1980.

Bishop, Robert, and Elizabeth Safanda. *A Gallery of Amish Quilts: Design Diversity from a Plain People*. New York: E.P. Dutton, 1976.

Brackman, Barbara. *An Encyclopedia of Pieced Quilt Patterns*. Paducah, Ky.: American Quilter's Society, 1993; originally published by Prairie Flower Publishing, 1984.

Central Oklahoma Quilters Guild. *Ultimate Illustrated Index to the Kansas City Star Quilt Pattern Collection*. Oklahoma City: 1990.

Goldberg, Rhoda Ochser. *The New Quilting & Patchwork Dictionary*. New York: Crown, 1988.

Malone, Maggie. *1001 Patchwork Designs*. New York: Sterling, 1982.

McCloskey, Marsha. *100 Pieced Patterns for 8" Quilt Blocks*. Seattle: Feathered Star Productions, 1992.

————. *Marsha McCloskey's Block Party: A Quilter's Extravaganza of 120 Rotary-Cut Block Patterns*. Emmaus, Pa.: Rodale Press, 1998.

McKim, Ruby Short. *101 Patchwork Patterns*. New York: Dover, 1962.

Rehmel, Judy. *The Quilt I.D. Book*. New York: Prentice Hall, 1986.

Stone, Clara. *Practical Needlework: Quilt Patterns*. Boston: C.W. Calkins and Co., 1906.

Block Index

*Author's note: I have found no blocks with identical piecing and/or value arrangements in the current literature, and therefore consider these to be original blocks. Generally, I've named them after my daughters and friends or after common features of Alaska, my home state. Zenobia's Puzzle is named for a fictional character—I wanted to include a block for every letter of the alphabet, and I needed a Z!

About the Author

Judy Hopkins is a prolific quiltmaker whose fondness for traditional design goes hand in hand with an unwavering commitment to fast, contemporary cutting and piecing techniques. Judy has been making quilts since 1980 and working full-time at the craft since 1985. Her primary interest is in multiple-fabric quilts; most of her pieces are inspired by classic quilts in a variety of styles. Her work has appeared in numerous exhibits and publications.

Writing and teaching are by-products of Judy's intense involvement in the process of creating quilts. She is author of *One-of-a-Kind Quilts*, *Fit To Be Tied*, *Around the Block with Judy Hopkins*, *Down the Rotary Road with Judy Hopkins*, and *Design Your Own Quilts* (a revised and updated version of *One-of-a-Kind Quilts*), and coauthor (with Nancy J. Martin) of *Rotary Riot*, *Rotary Roundup*, and *101 Fabulous Rotary-Cut Quilts*.

For the last several years, Judy has been working primarily from the scrap bag. Faced with a daunting accumulation of scraps and limited time to deal with them, she started looking for ways to apply quick cutting methods to scrap fabrics. This led to the design of Judy's popular ScrapMaster ruler, a tool for quick-cutting half-square triangles from irregularly shaped scraps, and the accompanying *Blocks and Quilts* for the ScrapMaster series.

Judy lives in Juneau, Alaska, with her husband, Bill, and their Labrador retriever. She has two grown daughters and four adorable and brilliant grandchildren who like to help her sew.